Disclaimer- I neit[her]... tru[e].

The graphic [content may no]t be appropriate for children under 16. It includes child and adult rape, abuse, assault, drugs, mental illness and torture. It's not for the faint of heart.

The story itself is a compilation of scenes, which give a small yet detailed glimpse into my life. Its viewpoints are not judgmental in nature although I'll share some opinions. I am merely giving my experience from my perspective, gathered through years of processing information inside the Etheric realms, collaborated by my conscious memories. It's evolved over time and will continue to do so, as more is revealed. The speculation of the intentions of the people involved were derived from their words and actions. I agree that the alleged crimes need further investigation. These are not facts; they are higher dimensional understandings of the bigger picture. Everyone is innocent until proven guilty. Obviously, there's more than one side to the story and I don't expect people to take my side or punish anyone. To be clear, I don't enjoy revealing fellow human's dark secrets, but if those responsible aren't going to, then I will. If they understood karma, they'd recognize the gift that it is. If you are person who finds yourself triggered by it, good. That's the first step towards healing.

Manipulated Memories

Dedicated to my family.
I have never been who you think I am.

Table of Contents

Disclaimer..1
Prologue...4
Chapter 1..8
Chapter 2...13
Chapter 3...20
Chapter 4...32
Chapter 5...53
Chapter 6...64
Chapter 7...71
Chapter 8...86
Chapter 9...99
Chapter 10..120
Chapter 11..142
Chapter 12..155
Chapter 13..185
Chapter 14..200
Chapter 15..213
Chapter 16..226
Chapter 17..240
Chapter 18..252
Chapter 19..268
Chapter 20..282
Conclusion..303
Survey..304

Prologue

Legends never die, they get reborn.
~ Campfire

As king of the gods, I had many responsibilities, none of which plagued me more than looking after the humans. A species I cared for deeply, as I'd had a hand in their upbringing in other lives. From the Mount Olympus throne room, I sat contemplating my growing concerns. Since their beginning, I tried protecting them from themselves, but watching their slow evolution was grueling.

After the original Titans were destroyed, I knew they'd one day return, and I wanted mankind to be ready, but it'd take time and careful planning to maneuver my ideas into place. So, I provided sacred knowledge to a chosen crowd of devotees. In hopes they'd spread the message of self-love and laws of the universe to the masses, but in return the concepts were stolen and ridiculed. My attempts to support them turned into fuel for wickedness. Religions were created and I faded into oblivion. My name was trampled, and I was portrayed as a wrathful god.

Manipulated Memories

Through a portal to their world, I watched as they ravaged each other. Fighting and stealing to gain wealth and power. It was clear, my messages hadn't reached them in time. They missed the entire point of incarnating into a collective world. With the chance to grow together and become a spacefaring race. They couldn't see the paradise they could've created. Instead, they chose death and ownership over bonding and collaborating. Imagine what Earth could've done without any borders.

I knew from experience that their world had been designed to allow free will. And I knew that when there are many choices available, there are those who will choose poorly. As the few vengeful souls took over the highest positions by force, I watched a new world be born. A world of jealousy, envy and strife, headed by the new Titans of the age. Earth became a place I couldn't blame the rest for despising.

Once that happened, the emotional baggage from the carnage began to hold them back from the peace they searched for. The information on how to release it was coveted and withheld on purpose. Used by some in power to extract lifeforce from the people, and it curdled my blood to watch as their children were being harmed in the process.

Earth was a mess.

As the new Titans reincarnated again and again, I sat resting my elbow on my seat arm with my forehead in one hand. Helplessly peering down on another war, my soul ached

Manipulated Memories

for them. I searched the sacred archives for a remedy that wouldn't break the rule to not interfere in the affairs of their people. After seeing no other choice, I decided that in the next life I'd shed my god form, descend into Earth, and become like them. I'd live a life that'd be seen as tragic and show the process of how to evolve past it. Even through the unthinkable.

It's been long awaited for this species to move to the next level, beyond the dark verses light ideologies. But for that to happen the truth can no longer be hidden.

And as I protected heaven's gate, in between lives, I finally heard the call. From the emptiness of space, a soft, androgynous voice whispered, "Earth needs help."

It was time to go to work.

To become human, I separated certain portions of the masculine and feminine molecules within me to fit into two bodies, and over time I'd send them more of our life force.

I searched for and found a suitable child candidate of a person being used by dark forces. Knowing she'd most likely have a life she couldn't handle. And together we made a unique soul contract for me to walk in and share her body until she couldn't handle anymore. Allowing my typically small magnetic field to grow over time. Making our evolution as painless as possible by helping me create energetic space to fill with consciousness once she left.

Manipulated Memories

It goes without saying that she'd get extra points from the big boss for helping with such an important mission. But it wasn't going to be without its challenges.

I left my partner with the responsibility to bring certain corrupt organizations' secrets to the public. As we said our heartbreaking goodbyes, he assured me he'd find me through the noise. And although that hasn't happened yet, I trust in his ability to fight the pull of the darkness.

From constant neglect, an illness had taken over the young body I was to inhabit, and she needed surgery. So, one day, she was sedated and dozed off to sleep. Giving me the perfect opportunity to drift through the veil of forgetfulness and into the shared space. When I woke up in human form, I remembered nothing of who I was or why I came here.

My name now is Morgan, born to a family in a coastal town in Oregon in 1985. Where the only constant in life was illusion and mistrust. Raised with three sisters in turbulent relationships and an unquenchable sibling rivalry. I never felt like they were my family, but as she was a part of me, they were part of me.

The truth is never as simple as we'd like it to be, and long-ago human nature was corrupted by a dark sludge of misconception. Entire family trees of thousands of years of lineage sit fruitless and decaying. Plagued by addiction and narcissism that rot and push the soul farther away from its person.

I'm glad to say that all of it can be reversed and all who even hold a sliver of soul within them can come home and enlighten to the godhood that is their birth right. When they learn they're the creators of this world and not the victims of it.

Step one for everyone is to read the room. If the problems you see are caused by everyone else, or the world…

Then the problem is you.

Chapter 1

All souls are immortal but the souls of the righteous are immortal and divine.
~Socrates

Since I felt out of place in the world, I saw myself as a team, and everyone else as my opponents. My team was either losing or winning, there was no in-between. You were either with me or against me, and I rarely recruited new members.

I never liked my name, but it had to do. With naturally light brown hair that growing up I dyed cherry red every month or so and I casually alternated face piercings depending on my mood. The tattoos on both my arms after eighteen, gave me an intense look, but I was empathetic and emotional.

The best way to explain how it felt to be me, was that it was painful to exist. Finding the right sentences seemed like a full-time job. My Gemini mind would sort through a list of appropriate responses, and my Libra rising would question it before picking the one you'd be comfortable with. It usually ended up being some part of the truth I thought you could handle.

Manipulated Memories

My fear was that if I said everything I thought, the world would banish me. Like my opinions weren't just less important, but actually harmful. That core belief forced me to censor myself.

Freckles lived just under my lower lashes and on my cheeks all year. I liked to do peace signs when I took pictures and laughed too loud. I giggled a lot, and it drove unhappy people crazy. My ego thought I was stronger than most girls, so I walked with a strut. I may have been short but not timid. I'll always be one of those overly happy and super alert morning people that, if you're not, you low-key hate.

But under the surface loomed a constant anxiety that wrapped itself around me like a snake, with its head on my chest. It whispered to me to be perfect, to smile and play happy even when I was drowning in emotion. It had me hold onto my feelings and opinions for so long that I exploded at random times, over seemingly insignificant things. Then I'd be left embarrassed and terrified of them even more.

I hid my pre-panic breathing with laughter and witty jokes. Pointing out your beautiful features or fresh hair cut to keep me in your good graces. Knowing good and well that every morning I felt forced to be on this planet. The dread of another day worn on my resting bitch face, that when you noticed turned into an envious grin because you didn't have my life.

Forensic files fascinated me, and death was never a scary thought. I didn't understand what beauty meant and fought with myself over the possibility I could have it. My weight fluctuated even as a small girl, and I noticed more than most.

Growing up I found inspiration through watching others. Mimicking their actions gave me an identity when I didn't have one. I was never the girl in high heels or small clothes, but I was jealous of the people who could. I usually wore a full face of makeup but never a red lip. My quiet need for attention was never bold but still all encompassing.

If I felt a need to enter your circle, I'd easily blend in. I didn't start conversations, but I would end them, and to argue with me was futile with my convictions.

As a young girl I was chronically sad that I wasn't the first choice, as my eldest sister Jera stole the show. Our mother told me to strive for perfection. "Look good and smile, and people will be good to you," she'd say. I gave that concept the middle finger and did what I wanted.

As I'm writing this, I live in Waikiki, Hawaii, a tropical paradise. One of the most incredible places I've ever seen. It reminds me of Venus, with dark skinned natives and luscious wildlife and scenery. Although it's one of approximately forty + places I've lived in the last few years. After being forced to run from state to state to keep my assailants guessing.

People can feel my psychic abilities when they meet me, whether they understand them or not. They begin asking questions, and I try to explain the multi-dimensional part of this reality, but it's lost in translation to most.

I learned that schizophrenia, a word they tried to throw at me a couple of times is a sign of extreme psychic gifts gone haywire. Too much connection to spirit can be debilitating and younger souls end up in hospitals unable to function. I found out it's a spiritual problem, not a mental malfunction. Luckily, I was able to cure myself with energy work, turning a life of struggle with forces I couldn't see into a connection with the spirit world that is nothing short of miraculous. In time, allowing me to interact with beings from other worlds, and travel the cosmos at will.

When you sit down to write a book as complex as this one, it's essential to consider your audience. Who might be interested in a story of conspiracy theories and multi-dimensional space travel? I imagine my readers to be intelligent, free thinkers who innerstand that what people portray on the surface has very little to do with who they are. And what you see manifested before you is only one part of a multi-layered existence.

I've spiritually watched my antagonists as they watch me for the last six years. Sometimes staring at the end of my driveway wondering. Will they storm my house and destroy my stuff? Will they lace my food and laugh at me while I'm terrified? What kind of day will it be today? And what about tomorrow? So, I sit here in my beautiful place in paradise and watch the trees sway and think.

Chapter 2

The image of God throws a shadow that is just as great as itself.

~C. G Jung

During my preschool years, my teacher noticed something strange about my behavior. She thought I'd said and done things in a sexual manner, when making comments and gestures. Which seemed out of place for such a small girl. Out of concern, she walked me to the principal's office and asked where I learned to act that way. Telling me I wasn't in trouble, but they needed to know where I learned such things.

With an innocent heart and fumbling words, I explained what was happening after I went to bed, with my stepfather. After the two paused and looked at each other, they hugged me. The principal picked up his phone and called his assistant requesting an appointment for me to see a therapist.

When I got home, my mom was already in a frenzy. "What did you tell them!" She yelled while shaking me. My eyes welled up with tears, staring at her in silence. She stepped back and forced her voice to calm. "What did you tell the principal, honey?" "That Jerry touched me right here," as I pointed towards my panties. Jerry groaned loudly from the living room sofa.

My mother turned and B-lined it towards him. He looked down, unable to deny it. She slapped him hard across the face. He tucked and rolled into the couch covering his head, overcome with shame.

My mother picked me up and set me on the stairs in between the living and dining room. She announced, "You can't have dinner or ice cream unless you take it back, Jerry wouldn't do that," and that I had to, "Stop being a liar, it must've been someone else." While Jera ran around me in circles, poking and singing, "Liar, liar, pants on fire."

I was crushed, and too young to argue, so I stomped my feet in frustration, refusing to do what she said. "It's not funny Morgan; you could get him in big trouble. He'll go away for a long time; is that what you want?" "No," I said, meaning it.

He was the only person in the house who was nice to me, he'd become my favorite person. Sure, he spanked us hard, and I hated that, but he was fun. He'd roll me up in the carpet and swing it around or put me on a sled tied to the back of a motorcycle in the back yard, in the snow. He was my everything at the time and I didn't want to lose him. Everyone he ever met loved him. But he also liked to party, and when people engage in that sort of thing, anything can happen.

Manipulated Memories

My body begged for my mother to soothe me, but I already knew she wouldn't. So, I anxiously put my fingers in my mouth, and stood confused at why she couldn't even look at me. And even though it wasn't abnormal, it was still heartbreaking. Jerry sat on the couch disheveled drinking a beer with his head in his hands.

My young, flustered mother who knew exactly what he'd been doing, walked past me as she cleaned the plates from everyone else's dinner. I didn't know what to say to make her not mad anymore. So, my mind made the executive decision to say I was wrong out of survival. To get the love I desperately craved. It twisted my internal compass from trusting myself towards believing others. A scar that would alter the rest of my life.

Jerry spent the next twenty-five years proving how sorry he was by being the best stepdad ever. Taking the entire family snowboarding, rollerblading and jet skiing. We were always having fun together and I thought of him as my hero, because my brain repressed the truth.

My mom had just had my youngest sister Kayla, the princess of the family by him when the school found out. So, getting me to forget what happened was key. She needed him around, at least for the time being.

At the appointment with the therapist, I denied he'd done anything wrong, and my case was never opened. But there was a bigger picture being developed that needed my mind primed in this way, for a plan waiting in the peripheral.

Manipulated Memories

The next day, the door opened in my kindergarten classroom, and two military-looking men in black suits appeared. I remember wondering if they were giants. My teacher pointed at me and motioned for me to speak with them. They led me into the hallway, and one bent down and pulled a red sucker from his breast pocket, offering it to me, while asking if I was brave. I shook my head yes, so he took my hand and said, "This'll hurt a little."

His partner reached into his jacket pocket then passed him a hand-sized device, that took blood from my finger. Within seconds the results were in, and he smiled after seeing the number 117 and O-. He asked if I wanted to meet a group of kids just like me, in an excited tone. The insinuation that I was special made that the best day of my life. His partner opened the classroom door and announced he'd be taking me for the rest of the day. Ending his statement in a hushed tone with, "Do not mark her as absent."

A woman met us at the car and locked me into a booster seat. We drove for hours, pulling up to a massive mansion in the middle of nowhere. Gardens of well-kept foliage surrounded a well-kept Victorian building.

Inside, groups of kids crowded the library studying ancient texts, while others played board games in one of the many hallways. A busy atmosphere of learning engulfed the environment. Everyone seemed content and energy of importance filled the air.

I took a tour of the place with a female teacher, who explained it was a secret school called The Elitest Academy.

Manipulated Memories

She kept asking me questions about my preferences, as we walked the halls. Like "What did I like to do for fun? What kind of hobbies was I into, and who was my favorite singer?" At that moment I felt loved for the first time. At home I was treated like a burden, but here, I was a valued commodity. Excitement permeated my entire body, and I couldn't stop grinning. This was what every kid dreams of, to be the center of attention.

My classmates consistently changed as kids were brought in from all over the world to train. On any regular day we learned things like magic and hand-to-hand combat. Soon, I found myself in love with gymnastics and thrived and excelled in it for many years.

Some of my first memories were of the preparations to be a part of the remote viewing project. Through meditation and visualization, we were taught to see into the unseen realms. So that as I got older, I could look for military and domestic targets out of reach of soldiers on the ground. In countries we were at war with or in buildings and caves impenetrable to humans. I would see not only murderers, rapists, and pedophiles but alien races and wars. Anyone our leaders needed to find could be a target.

It was a highly classified mission that could push the limits of our so called 'societal norms,' since they had no one looking over their shoulder. Secretly, their small but powerful, well-planned covert team worked silently, using all networks inside and outside the government, military, and occult.

Manipulated Memories

Their grooming process was treating us like kings and queens. I relished the food, candy, games, movies, dancing, and toys for the wealthy, unaware of the sick game surrounding me.

Every morning as we arrived, a nurse waited for us at the door, smiling and warmly offering hugs. Always asking the same three questions: "What kind of mood are you in today? Did anything negative happen at home last night?" And "What do you look forward to the most today?"

Depending on our answers she pushed either the yellow, red or green button on the small device that looked like a power meter. She'd set in on the top of one hand and we'd feel a brief pulse, like air being pushed through a straw, when it placed something under our skin. Although it was painless, I contemplated its purpose regularly.

Every so often we'd be taken into a medical room to be sedated and given electroshock therapy that had to have altered something in our brains. Because the more time I spent there the more my personality shrank. Eventually, I didn't speak unless spoken to and gradually morphed into a robot who'd take suggestions without fighting back.

I told them my favorite thing to do was watch the stars. So, they bought me a telescope and placed it on the roof. An instructor and I would lay and watch the movement of the night sky. They'd hand me a drink, and I'd sip and drift off. Waking up to feel something in my privates was abnormal, but mentally unable to place what happened.

Manipulated Memories

They mixed those encounters with making me feel important by asking me questions and wanting my opinions. Fortifying a deep connection to the leaders by filling my neglected heart.

We lived for short periods in a dormitory, ate, and studied together like college kids. They made us believe we were warriors and taught us to fight with our minds and bodies as if we were superhuman soldiers. Constantly begging us to never tell anyone, claiming we were so special no one would understand. Threatening that if we did, we couldn't come back.

One Saturday at the end of class, I was asked by a teacher, "Did you have a good day today?" My young critic replied, "I didn't like the games I had to play with the boys; they touched my privates." He responded with, "That's okay honey, you don't have to worry about that, it won't happen again." As I looked up at him, he pulled out a small pen and donned blue sunglasses. "Look right here for me," as he pointed towards the top. A small flash burst from the device, and my awareness stunned. I looked up to see his smiling face as he handed me my bag and jacket. He reminded me about how much fun I had learning to bake cookies that day.

Within a couple of years, I heard about the experiments. When I asked, the other kids told me horror stories. But it didn't matter, by then I was willing to do whatever they wanted. Scared to complain or seem ungrateful by questioning it. Sadly, I naively trusted them, and since they said it was good for me, I believed them.

Manipulated Memories

A whiteboard displaying accomplishments sat in the entryway, and at six years old, it was bigger than I was. Each kid's name was on the left, with a list of code names for tests on the right. A star meant completed, and an X needed to retake. I was curious and contemplated the mystery.

The lessons and subject matter were far from ordinary. But it was too exciting to get caught up with the specifics of things. For that reason, I kept my thoughts to myself and said little else. I wanted to be perfect and would do whatever I had to, to get people to think I was.

Chapter 3

Children don't get traumatized because they are hurt.
They get traumatized because they are hurt and alone.
~ Gabor Mate

Two years later, on an overcast and drowsy winter morning, my teacher at Elitest briefed my class about the testing procedures for the first time. I remember gripping my pencil hard and watching as my fingers turned red while my mind suggested I be brave. She encouraged us to support each other and reminded us we were being trained for excellence. We all looked at each other with fear and excitement as we got up from our seats to be escorted into the elevator in silence. There wasn't time to worry about what was going to happen next, since we knew we'd been being prepared for this for the last two years.

The sound of the heavy metal scraping along the building tinged something in me, triggering a warning feeling I couldn't heed. I wanted to grab one of my friend's hands and tell him I was scared but I just stared at the door.

Manipulated Memories

As the lowering momentum abruptly halted, my stomach dropped. The gears in the door took their sweet time revealing the rotting wood smell of the basement. A spotlight beamed from the ceiling towards a platform in the middle of the location. My hypervigilance scanned the perimeter and noticed that the outer rim of the room was filled with animal cages. Within a few steps, I was hit with a foul odor of feces that assaulted my nostrils. No doubt coming from the lion, alligator, and panther that made little noise when we entered the room.

The group gathered on the handmade deck in the center, next to a large above ground pool. In front of a wooden chair that sat at its edge. On one side of its frame sat a Frankenstein looking lever attached to some kind of mechanism. Everyone was trying to figure out what was going on and the quiet gave us time to run through different scenarios in our heads.

After a few minutes of contemplation, the testing instructor named Phillip motioned that I'd be the first to go with a flick of a finger. My teammates cheered me on as I stepped up to the seat. My body was belted in with thick leather straps by the class's assistant. Two folded in opposite directions over my calves, one around each forearm, one hugged to my stomach, and one held my forehead to the back of the chair with more pressure than necessary.

In a rhythmic tone Phillipe explained that the contraption I was bound to was a torture device meant to gain intel from our enemies. I rolled my eyes with attitude and chuckled at the chaos of it. At that point, I had to put on a brave face, but everyone else looked like they wanted to throw up.

The assistant gave no warning as he reached for and grabbed the lever pulling it as hard as he could, sending my seat hurling backwards. Dunking the top half of my torso into the water. I let out a yelp as my head hit the water first. It reached the top of my shoulders in seconds as I floated just under the surface. My eyes burned as I tried to see through it. A calmness went over me, and I thought about death, far less scared than I should've been.

Bubbles escaped my mouth and nose, and time stopped. I watched each one hit the surface in slow motion. Like the intensity of the absurdity peeled back reality itself. The rickety chair screeched as it forced me back up into the stench of the world. My body involuntarily screamed. But as I hit the water again my senses relaxed, and as I was brought to the surface again fear arose. Almost like death was the easier option of the two. Every muscle ached from the clenching, and my lungs burned. I could barely get two breaths in between and by the third one I was convinced death was my fate. The shock caused me to panic but again I was lowered. It felt like I spent centuries going back and forth between worlds, until, thankfully, I was lifted out. My classmates cheered for me like a hero and congratulated me with hugs and high fives on the first of many stars.

For the sake of time, and my sanity, I won't go into the details about all the different tests. Trying to portray the depth of intensity that we experienced wouldn't be possible anyway. Part of me wants to say that we lost our innocence during these experiences. But I've since learned that the projects minions don't pick innocent children. They need a certain type of home life to be present before a candidate is qualified. For girls' intelligence was highly regarded and for boys' strength was revered. In either instance sexual exploitation had to have taken place prior to the child being brought in. There are many reasons that a child who had suffered those types of mistreatments at home would be better suited. One being a need for attention and willingness to go against their own morals to get it. Another being that their brains were more malleable because they hadn't formulated a sense of self yet. With conflicting emotional damage, a child could more easily become able to separate their consciousness to keep itself safe. Since the mind and body both have protective mechanisms that fall into place after a threshold of trauma incurs.

They did include things like being held over the pool with an alligator biting at our heels and being stood in a corner with a lion standing a few feet from us, growling and swatting, only missing by inches. Once as a group we were even injected with narcotics and placed in a labyrinth in the backyard, accompanied by hostel images and eerie noises. Which unsurprisingly made most kids freeze or go into psychotic fits. While others would sit staring at the walls for hours.

In the beginning, during some of them, the intensity of the fear caused screaming, terror and desperation. My entire body would tremble, and every cell would search for something to soothe it. This'd be when someone would come over with a needle and extract my adrenochrome filled blood. But as I got older and more able to handle the discomfort this happened less and less.

There wasn't any way to prepare for these events and eventually I went numb and even at times welcomed the pain. The praise we received was addictive, because it made me feel invincible and powerful. The agony became acceptable after years of it, and we convinced ourselves they were helping us become superheroes.

But behind the scenes was a bigger plan being executed. A long game strategy, that counted on the fact that as I experienced so much pain early on, it short circuited the wiring of my pleasure and pain sensors. Convincing my energetic system to aim towards discomfort. Which was exactly what they wanted, because it caused me to be able to run towards danger when they needed me to and more likely to destroy myself as I got older.

Two years later as I walked back from lunch towards my classroom, another instructor named Tyler stopped and ordered me into an empty remote viewing room. I hesitantly picked a seat and put on the headphones hanging on the wall, noticing the screen in front of me. He sat beside me and instructed, "It will be over soon, as long as you watch the entire thing." I nodded.

A film began of two men raping a dark-haired girl. I could tell she was awake but unable to move, she didn't speak but dread shown through her bulging glossy eyes. The men enjoyed the experience more than anything I'd ever seen. Giddy and enthralled with themselves while cackling with expressive movements. They slowly but brutally ripped off her arms and legs one at a time, and even as a child, I knew it was real.

Through my headphones I could hear faint words being said that I couldn't make out, but I could tell they were repeating by the tempo. I looked at Tyler and pointed at my ears. He mouthed "It's fine," and pointed towards the screen.

I didn't know it but the commands I was hearing were finalizing their diabolical procedure. My mind was learning how to set up and switch into two personalities. Although the effects would take time to manifest, I was being programmed to transfer the memories of the C.I.A associations to the other identity. Ultra soldier Mia-369 was officially created and was now being incubated, a side of myself I wouldn't see unless activated. They had successfully, at least for a while, protected themselves and their precious data.

Step one had been easy, get my loyalty. Now they were birthing a new person (or so they thought) that would listen without defiance. But that wasn't going to be as simple as they wanted it to be.

What they didn't know was that before this life I knew what was going to happen to us. They believed they had taken the stronger personality and could use her to destroy me when they needed to. But they had made one very vital error in their plan, because they didn't know who they were messing with. They have underestimated me in a way that they won't come back from.

A bleed through of Mia's experiences did happen from time to time, which'd seem like dreams or intrusive thoughts. And I know that you're curious about her missions with the projects, but for now that information will have to wait. This series has a lot to divulge about many things and I won't be giving all the details all at once, for many reasons. For now, we proceed with Morgan's experience. Mia was only taken out for small trips and specific jobs anyway, and in time I will tell you all about them.

Another two years went by, and I was pulled out of class and into a conference room where a group of men sat and asked me a million questions. Things like: Do you hear other people's thoughts? Do you feel other people's pain? Weird stuff I'd never considered, I answered the best I could.

Someone told me later they were from a secret society called the Illuminati, recruiting new members. Since it was ninety percent male, I would be privileged to be a part of it, they said. I'd never heard of such a thing, so I asked a bunch of questions. They just smiled and chuckled to themselves. "You'll have to wait and see for yourself."

A couple years went by, and Tyler again grabbed me from class. Escorting me down the administrative hallway which students weren't allowed to be in, and into a bleak white interrogation room with a small table and two chairs opposite each other. He motioned for me to sit and I picked a chair, shaking with anticipation. My head was spinning with the questions I knew better than to ask. Scanning the room with my eyes, I waited for what felt like a lifetime tapping my fingers on the cold metal tabletop.

Finally, someone opened the door, and a man walked in with a manilla folder. He slammed it on the table and said, "We need you to read someone for us." "Read someone?" "Yes, tell us if he's lying." He set down a pen and opened the folder. Inside was a checklist with twenty questions and a truth or deception column on the right. He instructed me sternly, "Don't speak to him other than to ask the questions, you got it?" I shook my head in agreement.

He brought in a heavy-set man about forty years old with a beard and receding long brown hair. Sitting him across from me, Tyler left the room, and we were alone together. I smiled and tried to seem cordial knowing that the instructors wouldn't like it, because my rebellion even then knew no bounds.

It was clear life had weathered his face with lines of sadness, and he couldn't hide the worry in his eyes. We shook hands, and I explained that I needed to ask him some questions. He nodded, and we began. "Did you tell your family about your relationship with the C.I.A?" He answered a quick "No," which I knew was telling. I could see he was sweating and feel his heart racing. My intuition told me he was lying, and I checked the appropriate box. We continued down the line of questions, and I felt for him; he was lying most of the time.

Manipulated Memories

What I didn't know was that the leaders already knew the answers. The real test was for me, a way for the Illuminati to see my value. My accuracy would solidify my position in becoming a member. Whether I wanted to or not.

Tyler came back in and grabbed the man by the arm. He motioned for me to follow, and I trailed behind. We walked down the colorless hallway about a hundred feet until we stopped at the elevator. Tyler pointed toward the opening doors, and I walked in first. After two floors, the doors opened into a small unlit corridor. To my surprise, we turned left heading into an area I'd never been before. It was musky and smelled of smoke. I could barely see except for a few small red and white lights across the large open room. My eyes struggled to make out the other five people's silhouettes already there. The intensifying smell gagged my throat, and I couldn't hold back a painful cough.

In the center of the frigid room stood an engraved ceremonial seven-foot-long table standing three feet tall. A glint shined from the plastic lining covering the surface. On the ground, a black plastic bucket was placed underneath the far end, sitting just outside a design painted in white on the floor of an upside-down five-pointed star. Uneven rows of black and white, thick and thin, tall and short candles lined the walls, and chills ran down my spine. My intuition told me to run, but I was paralyzed by fear. I could sense the presence of something evil and I knew, it knew I was there.

I asked to leave, and Tyler said to stand exactly where I was, about ten feet away, inside a white box with a symbol that meant sacrifice drawn on the floor. He pushed the scruffy man on the table as he begged for his life. Unable to predict what would happen next, I sat on the ground and held my legs in my arms. The other men gathered around and cuffed his arms in straps and tied them under the table. Then tied a rope around his feet. He urgently pleaded and promised he wouldn't tell anyone else, assuring them he'd only told his wife.

After Tyler spoke some strange words in Latin, the screaming began. Deep, hard, wailing pain reverberated like thunder off the walls in sync with his breath. Only seconds in between the silence and agony. I looked over at precisely the wrong time and saw them joker style cut his mouth from lip to ear on both sides. My stomach felt queasy, and I threw up all over the floor. I couldn't hold back my fear any longer, and I started whimpering.

I hunched onto all fours and pushed myself off the ground, turning and running towards the door as fast as I could. But I barely made three lunges when someone grabbed me by the arm, pulled me back to where I was before, and told me to stay. I curled up on the ground and kept my head on my knees and my fingers in my ears until the noise stopped. Rocking back and forth, whispering to myself, "This is my fault."

When the room fell quiet, I saw a drain spout on the table pouring blood into the bucket. Each man filled a cup as it streamed down in spurts. They cheered and said something in Latin I didn't understand. Each took a drink and poured the rest out on top of the dead body. I held my stomach to make sure I didn't puke again. My entire body was shaking and on fire from the adrenaline. My mind raced with thoughts like: Why was this allowed to happen? What kind of people would do this? What were they going to do to me?

When it was all over, Tyler grabbed me by the arm. Looked at me directly in the eye and said in a monotone slow rhythm.

"Please don't bother telling anyone. They wouldn't believe you anyway. You are going to work for us, and we will ask you to do things, and if you're good at your job, you'll be greatly rewarded. This is a part of our religion. He was a sacrifice to Satan. He gives us power. You can have this power too. I know this was hard to see, but you'll get used to it. It doesn't happen all the time, but it is necessary. The pain you feel inside Satan can take away. All the problems at home and school will be gone forever. Would you like that?"

I shrugged and put my head down, scared to give the wrong answer. He slowly and gently lifted my head with his index finger and asked again, "Do you?" "Yes," I mumbled. Knowing that, saying no wasn't an option. I did want the problems at home and school to go away. I wanted to feel powerful, and I didn't want what I just saw to happen to me.

He forced me to make a deal with the devil at that moment. That spiritually was real, even if I didn't mean it. It was official, I was going to be indoctrinated into a world of power, greed, and lust by force. There'd never be an easy way out.

Chapter 4

Demons are like obedient dogs; they come when they are called.

~ Remy De Gourmont

Three years later, on a Monday, at 11:15 am I sat twirling a plastic braided choker, trying to stay awake. Staring at a computer wondering why I was in such a stupid school. My old principal put me in the city's alternative schoolhouse after I refused to attend my freshman classes. I couldn't help that I felt claustrophobic sitting in a classroom, and the social ranking system of popularity that littered the halls made me sick.

As my train of thought continued, I contemplated what my mom had said the night before, "Are you sure you want to wear that, it makes you look chubby." As she pointed at my favorite Tommy Hilfiger puffy vest. I begrudgingly spoke to her in my head, like she was right in front of me. For one, it was a puffy vest, and for two, who says that to their kid?

Manipulated Memories

I kept looking at my stomach that wasn't flat but wasn't bulging. Until that comment, I didn't know there was anything wrong with it. With one sentence, she'd unlocked a new insecurity in me. Now I'd hyper focus on even the smallest details of my body.

During the same time, I'd fallen in love with an older troublemaker. Normally I'd skip class before 2nd period, and we'd smoke weed and walk around the two-lane town looking for trouble. But the school figured me out and sent me here. To a hole in the wall makeshift building with three rooms, set up in between retail shops in the middle of town. That looked like an old computer store. Full of kids with disabilities and learning issues. The teachers treated me like a child, and the homework was so easy it made me crazy. I didn't want to talk, and it was sarcastic and unreasonable when they forced me to.

Someone called me into the office to take a phone call. As I picked up the receiver, I heard a specific sentence and switched personalities. Two men in black suits walked into the office and nodded their heads towards the front door. One broke off to the left to get the car. The other pointed towards the parking lot. They didn't need to say anything; I knew why they were there.

A black S.U.V. pulled up in the front of the school, and I jumped in without struggle. We drove for around two hours until we got to the gate I dreaded, and my stomach dropped. I lowered my head to hide the look of revolt. As the steel bars opened, the car slowly rolled into the exquisitely manicured

Manipulated Memories

lawn. I barely noticed the rose bushes decorating the perimeter. But I did make a mental note that the long driveway looked like something out of the Alice in Wonderland movie. The entire panorama appeared pristine and clean, but I knew better. The darkness and secrets inside festered on the walls, casting a shadow on the postcard image.

We arrived at the academy's marbled stairs where a man in a blue suit stood with one arm behind his back. I got out and greeted him. As we walked inside, he briefed me, "Mark Skrunton, originally from Orlando, on the run for weapons dealing, time is of the essence with this guy because he has friends that could help him go underground. We need to find him quickly." He handed me a manilla folder, I looked through and glimpsed the picture. On the way, we passed the electroshock therapy room, where my friend Jordan was about to be hit with a powerful current. I shuddered, turning my face away with disgust.

The long hallway was met by two clear glass doors that opened automatically. My escort left me to get dressed in the locker room, and I changed into my all-black military-looking uniform and headed to the office. I slowly made my way into the remote viewing section. Where a small classroom was split into five booths with headphones on the left and an intercom on the right. The walls around me nearly glowed from the green translucent glass.

I picked station three to sit and study the contents of the folder. The description said he was a thirty-year-old escaped convict. I put on the headphones so they could send high frequency waves to empower my psychic gifts, allowing my brain to slow. I closed my eyes and concentrated on the picture.

I followed the regular training procedures, step by step, like a good soldier would. Asking spirit to take me to him in his current position on this planet in this timeline. I felt energy shift around me through my senses and heard words from the vibration of space itself. It pulled me towards him and described the surrounding area. I recorded that he was somewhere in Arizona. At a campsite with barely any supplies, cold and hungry. I gave details about the camp's layout, including mountains behind him and a lake nearby. Enough information for them to find him. When I got home that night, I looked at my mom for a long time, studying the wildness of her. I knew I'd forget what happened when I went to sleep, and I wanted to sit in knowing of it with her in the room for a while. It was the only power I had in her presence. She didn't ask where I was, and she wouldn't the next time. I calculated different possibilities that could make someone so selfish. Trauma, abandonment, entitlement or vanity. The child in me wanted to run up and hug her, professing my undying love. But the teenager I'd become wanted to walk up and punch her in the face. Force her to hear about the things I knew about the world that she didn't. I felt sorry that she was content (or seemed to be) with an emotionally empty home, just because her bank account was doing well. I said to myself "I never want to be like her, money makes people shallow."

Manipulated Memories

I thought about the things I did at the academy, about how if we didn't have work we practiced different physical arts. Everything from Tai Chi to dance and energy manipulation. Even the men did ballet to gain stamina and grace. Or school to learn topics that'd come into play later, like ancient religions and symbolism. And how the curriculum sculpted timid and docile personalities while hiding intelligence to make us seem weak and helpless. Creating weapons enemies wouldn't recognize.

I noticed that when we became teenagers, the mission shifted. A part of me begged for my mom to notice that now I was beginning to use my new skills in the real world. Sometimes sent to parties and gatherings of elite organizations. Fancy ballrooms or pool parties for the rich and famous who loved children. Let's not be coy about what I was dealing with; they were pedophiles and degenerates with large amounts of money and high security clearances.

I sat paralyzed by my life's secrecy, staring at the door to the room my mother was in. Knowing that most of the time, I wouldn't remember the assignments afterwards. My heart ached for the part of me that went home enraged that the world didn't make sense. Knowing her life felt bleak and hopeless and yet unable to fully understand why. She thought the world was full of lifeless show-offs who couldn't have a meaningful conversation. She craved structure and routine but never got any, so I knew her rebellious nature would grow.

Manipulated Memories

I didn't always know what she was up to without me. But I did know how she felt. And when her first love said he couldn't see us anymore, for our own good, all bets were off. I knew it was the projects doing, because if we were around someone too much, they'd get suspicious about where we were going when it was time to train. So we weren't allowed to date very long. I was programmed not to have interest in that sort of thing, so it didn't bother me the same way. I tried to hint to her what was happening through her writings, but she didn't have the information to tie it to. I gave up after a while and buckled in for her earned angry phase.

The more depressed she got the more frustrated I became, and neither of us cared about school or doing the right thing anymore. We began stealing money from our mom's husband by sneaking in his room and grabbing a couple twenties off his unnecessarily large stack of cash. Using it to buy drugs and party with friends. Our body insecurities went into overdrive and life became the new enemy.

After getting kicked out of our mom's house for missing too much school, we moved back in with our father. A smart con meant to get us closer to Fort Lewis. We lived on the one decent street in the not-so-great part of a small town, that smelled like fish from a papermill. Morgan spent her nights out with the older boys in the trailer park down the street, as a professional troublemaker follower. Eating scraps and looking for petty crimes that could make enough money for a twenty sack to dull the pain of existing.

Manipulated Memories

While I worked my ass off for the projects now that I was out of school. The more they asked of me the more I questioned the entire deal. They kept saying I was not only helping the country but the world. That the things I was doing were part of a bigger plan to rid the world of gangsters and terrorists, but none of it added up. Morgan shouldn't have to be so miserable for them to get what they needed done. It started to feel like her and I's misery was part of the show. But I couldn't prove it.

Later that same year, right after I turned sixteen, my instructor called her and gave the command to switch. He informed me we were going to one of the secret science department locations called MI Lab and suggested I pack a bag. I told my dad I'd be with friends for the weekend, and he didn't even look up from his newspaper, just grumbled okay in response.

A black S.U.V pulled up to our house and I closed the front door with a sad feeling. Wishing my dad would wonder where I was going, or who I was with. I thought to myself, "If he only knew."

The vehicle had Damien, a ten-year-old classmate that wasn't around much and twelve-year-old Jordan plus a handler inside. They told me we were going on a private jet, and we drove to the tarmac and took our seats in silence. Jordan sat next to me and held my hand most of the trip, even though we were in soldier mode.

Our group was met by two uniformed guards when the plane landed on the runway in Houston, who took us to a

Manipulated Memories

concealed underground train station. Locked with scanners on each door with retinal recognition and protected by what could only be the security of the future everywhere.

A shuttle took us to a conference room, where we were briefed on the base's purpose. My curiosity was piqued when they said it was an experimental unit meant to find and test new technologies.

The group was brought into a room with three five-inch dark grey disks covering the floor. After aiming a remote at the ground, it turned on three alien holographic images to stand life-size in front of us. The instructor began educating us on each one, then compared them to humans, by opening the bodies in the middle exposing their insides.

He explained their diet, preferences in weather, and pointed out if we had similarities. With a laser, they highlighted each organ in a brief description. Starting with the non-threatening species and moving their way to the more dangerous ones.

It seemed to me like they came up with a narrative to fit their judgmental bias. Picking and choosing what to say about which race. Tailoring our minds to accept and dismiss certain information. I could tell they wanted us to fear and not fear certain races. As a highly impressionable teenager, I took in their words like air.

I remember them saying something about working with the reptilians on our military's security. Leaving out that they try to rule the world, obviously. They both cautioned us to stay away as we are a food source and insisted that they wouldn't harm us without reason. After the lesson, they took us to see the bodies of a few of the class subjects. At the end of the class, and to all of our surprise, it was time to meet one of the most dangerous beings in existence.

The second I came into contact with the green, blue and yellow, nine-foot tall, muscular reptilian with wings, I felt every hair on my body stand up. His skin glistened from the iridescent color, with a texture like a cross between a turtle and an alligator. As he spoke to me telepathically, my muscles paralyzed. While casually sitting in his throne-like chair, he didn't look at me when saying, "You don't have to fear me today."

I would've peed my pants if I weren't around a bunch of people. To this day, it was the most intimidating encounter I ever had. When he spoke to me, it was like a god had taken over my mind and tried to coerce me into submission. I wasn't aware of the implant in my brain that translated his alien speech into English. It vibrated through my brain, making loud hissing noises that stopped me in my tracks. My eyes widened, and I couldn't respond.

I was on the verge of a nervous breakdown just being in the same room, and now, I wanted to turn and run, but my guardians noticed and said, "Everything is fine." I had no choice but to stay and Jordan and Damien seemed almost entranced by him, and I sensed that his power was attractive to them.

The adults had a brief conversation where he expressed concern that they could make sure I wouldn't become a problem, and my instructor assured him I wouldn't. They reiterated that they had something planned to make sure of it. He left them with the understanding that he would be making sure they succeeded.

A short time later, we were taken into a windowless office about a hundred feet away. I recognized the remote viewing room immediately because it was similar to ours on base. The three of us were handed folders and told to join the group. We each picked seats to look over the paperwork.

This time the target was a group of men they called a dangerous cult. Our instructions were to find a particular vehicle adorned with a satellite receiver. After we jotted down what information we could find, we were done, and it was time to leave.

Damien and Jordan sat next to me in the car. With a desire to protect the boys, I asked out loud, "Where are we going now?" Our handler announced, "To a hotel for the night. Does that sound fun?" "Yeah!" We all replied loudly in unison. And I could relax momentarily because we were done for the day. With a smile, Damien asked, "Does it have a pool?" "No," the driver lied, in a tone of voice that said, don't ask me again.

We used the back entrance to sneak into our four-star hotel room suite. I blurted out, "There's no way this place doesn't have a pool." Our chaperone dropped our bags on the floor, ignoring me, and said, "Dial #1 on the phone for dinner." We looked at each other with exhilaration, and the boys both said "Yes!" in unison. I laughed.

Manipulated Memories

After stuffing our faces with cheeseburgers and fries, we were tired. So we all snuggled on the king size bed. In the middle of the night, I felt Damien's hands exploring my body. Annoyed, I pushed him away and fell back to sleep, secretly flattered. The following day a call told us to get ready by ten. The S.U.V. waited at the door, and we scampered in. Our bags were brought around and thrown into the back.

We drove for thirty minutes until we got to a small gate surrounding a large rectangular, blue and white glass building. From the outside, it looked completely deserted.

Inside the main door was a security check like a courthouse. A conveyor belt took our personal metal items. While a scanner searched for weapons as we passed through. On the other side, each of us were handed visitor badges to put around our necks.

The group was slowly guided towards an elevator, where someone pushed the T button. After a long time, it opened into a science lab. A large open sterile white room had been constructed around a ball of mercury encased in something clear, sitting on a stand three feet off the ground, surrounded by machines and monitors.

In the middle of the room sat an observation area with more computers surrounded by glass. In front of the metal object sat a single chair, where I was ordered to sit, but I became nervous and grumbled "I don't want to." "Sit," my handler said. "What's it going to do to me," "It's going to tell us your future," he casually said, like it was no big deal.

Manipulated Memories

The blood in my face drained and I stared at Jordan in suspense. A technician placed two medical pads on my forehead and attached them to wires. Then adhered individual finger cuffs and straps to secure my ankles. I nudged around to see how secure it was, knowing I couldn't get out.

Excitement to see the future was met with fear something bad would show up. If there's one thing that followed me through life it was a constant feeling that the end of the world was right around the corner. And in that moment, I wondered if that was what I would see.

I heard a soft buzzing sound, and light emitted from the metal ball. Swishing noises encircled me, and blue, white, green, and purple lights slowly swelled around the object. Creating a cube of what looked like swirling water about five feet around. The doctor finished and asked all five other people to enter the observation chamber. He took my hand and said, "This won't hurt; I promise." Which calmed me a little.

As the doctor watched a screen through the glass, I sat entranced in the lights. The rushing noises continued to get louder until, to my surprise, it fell silent. A glowing transparent ribbon between me and the ball encircled the cube. When it crescendos up to its full potential, the lights turn into colors on a self-made screen. Fuzzy still frames began to morph into better quality in real time, playing a scene recorded by someone's eyes. Within a couple minutes, the pixilation cleared into a high-definition reenactment. A group of people protesting outside the white house began to show. Picket signs and shouting were all saying the same thing. We want disclosure!

It was frustrating that I couldn't hear the details. What is disclosure? Disclosure of what? The operator of the image turned to its right, where a blonde-haired, blue-eyed man stood holding their hand and chanting together. I turned back to the observation room to see Jordan puzzled. I put together that they looked oddly similar, and he knew it. The video began to move forward and backward in time.

Showing a court proceeding with hundreds of people waiting outside, and a trip on a spaceship to multiple other worldly locations. With glimpses of non-humanoid beings in military uniforms, and riots in the streets.

In my head I thought, there's no way this could be real, right? I heard loud angry talking from the adults behind me, and that could only mean one thing. I was in trouble for things that hadn't even happened yet. Great.

Next up was Damien. I took his hand and told him it didn't hurt. He looked at me and said, "I'm tough, I can handle it." His life was maneuvered through like a video game. First, the Mk-ultra program was blasted onto the screen, illustrating his training to be a killer. Then his deployment in the Army during a war with suffering and tragedies that had tears running down my face, but he sat cold and emotionless. Followed by some kind of ceremony where blood dripped down his back from self-inflicted wounds by a leather handle with frayed pieces of fabric limped towards the ground. And finally, a visit while in prison with a female who looked like me, only older. I cupped my hands over my mouth, trying not to scream.

When it was Jordan's turn, he fought the handler who tried to get him in the chair, getting away for a moment. He ran to me and grabbed my hand pleading, "I don't want to see it." I hated that I couldn't protect him, "I know it, be strong, and it will be over soon." I hugged him and calmly whispered, "They can't take your heart." A saying I had come up with to ease him through our adventures together.

His show began with his family fighting intensely. He lowered his head and closed his eyes. Then it moved to him as a young adult in a bunker in the middle of the desert with six other men in uniforms, hooked to head wires and heart monitors. He peaked at the screen to see himself getting an I.V while sitting in a wheelchair, dirty and lifeless. After that, he refused to open his eyes, and I didn't blame him. I saw him marry and have a baby before they turned the machines off.

They didn't seem to take as much time or care as much about what showed up for the boys. My guess is that they knew they could change it.

As we went to leave, our handler pulled out a memory swipe. He smiled at each of us before temporarily blocking our short-term memory. After they made up a story about our tour through the science lab, it was time to go home. We headed to the airport without any stops. Inside the car was silent and eerie, as our brains adjusted to the new information.

Manipulated Memories

Since it was now imperative that I didn't become that person in the future, they had to do something to alter my timeline. So I was forced into a small medical office and hooked to an electric shock therapy machine and given a shot in the arm. I fell asleep almost instantly. And like writing code for a computer, they programmed commands straight into my brain.

"You will not shower regularly or take care of yourself physically."
Burst
"You will be raped repeatedly."
Burst
"No one is safe."
Burst
"You will struggle with money."
Burst
"Your boyfriends will cheat with your sisters."
Burst
"Everyone is against you."
Burst
"You can't trust your memories."
Burst
"The world isn't safe."
Burst

After I was removed from the table and taken to my room, Damien was brought in and told to lay on the table. After he was sedated, the handler whispered in Latin, moving his hands around like a magician. Pulling a red transparent female sex demon with wings and tentacles out of thin air, that floated into Damien. In English, he began to speak with authority…

"You are the strongest man alive."
Burst
"Everyone is jealous of you."
Burst
"They want to take what you have."
Burst
"No one is as powerful as you."
Burst
"You are secretly attracted to men."
Burst
"Sex is the only thing that makes life worth living."
Burst
"You are obsessed with and hate Morgan at the same time."
Burst

Damien was awakened and Jordan was called in to have the same experience with different commands.

"Women are toys for you to play with."
Burst
"You own this world."

Manipulated Memories

Burst

"You are the most beautiful man to ever exist."

Burst

"Feelings don't matter."

Burst

"You are obsessed with money and power."

Burst

"Trust no one."

Burst

"People will hurt you."

Burst

"You are secretly homosexual."

Burst

"You love Morgan but are terrified of her."

Burst

For insurance that I wouldn't have anyone to ally with, my sister Jera was picked up from school and brought in to have the same procedure. They used our past to guarantee we'd become enemies in the future. I'm not sure I'll ever get her back.

"You hate Morgan, she is your enemy."

Burst

"You sleep with Morgan's boyfriends for fun."

Burst

"Morgan's weak."

Burst

"Morgan's an embarrassment to your family."
Burst
"Morgan doesn't deserve to be alive."
Burst

This experience tailored our thoughts and decisions by unknowingly repeating through our subconscious minds.

A couple months later, Jordan and I were pulled into a conference room. Where an instructor placed a stack of papers on the table and opened it with one life changing statement, "We have come to make a deal." Jordan was too young to understand what the contract said, and I was too rebellious to make good decisions. I'm still unclear about how much our parents knew.

As the intensity of the tests grew, both my personalities were unwilling to participate. The acts we did got suspiciously seedier, and the fun turned into forced entertainment. The lack of emotion caused me to doubt their motives, and someone noticed I wanted out.

After spending incredible amounts of money training me, it would've been a waste to lose me this early in life. Plus I'm sure they wanted more data for the mind control methods.

So, they came up with a plan that promised me a better life. Where I didn't have to come into the office anymore. But I should've known there was a catch in their sadistic chess game. They showed me a contract for $300,000 if I agreed to their terms. But if I'd read the paperwork, I would've seen they planned to take my memories. It was a scam, but I was given a week to consider the offer.

It turns out they couldn't continue the experiments without my permission, because spiritual contracts had to be agreed to in order to take their full effect. Even now I'm impressed with the level of intelligence I was dealing with. They knew exactly what they were doing, and I didn't stand a chance.

The Illuminati leaders began inviting me to their homes and parties, showing me a lavish life I could only dream of at that point. Hinting that I could afford this lifestyle one day if I signed the papers. They said twenty years goes by in the blink of an eye, and then this could all be mine. I walked in the backdoors to attend their balls and smoking parlor card games with the wealthiest people in the world. Where they portrayed a PG-13 lie until midnight. The opulence, laughter and dancing allured many to whatever that was, but the truth was an evil I was too immature to recognize. If I'd known, I would've run as fast as I could in the other direction.

At the academy there wasn't room for opinions, and the more questions I asked about the subjects, the more I was shunned by the group. I was fed up and couldn't keep my mouth shut about wanting out, but I was torn, because the terms of the contract were harsh. I'd have to erase my memories of the project and the Illuminati association. Then agree to be sexually and emotionally assaulted on an unknown number of occasions. I didn't want to think about

Manipulated Memories

what they meant by that. My mind was already so gullible I let them convince me I could gain power from the process without recalling the events. An idea that sounds good in theory but was clearly morally flawed.

I thought long and hard about which decision to make, going back and forth with the pros and con's list I'd created. Did I want to suffer in the future, no, but could I handle living in two different worlds as a spy, no way. I was emotionally exhausted by it all. After a few talks with different project members, I weighed the evidence and took their offer. Learning the hard way that trauma stays with you whether you remember it or not.

The next morning group members showed up to my house and I snuck out and met them on the road, where an S.U.V. waited. Thankfully for me, I wasn't the sentimental type and letting go of things had become natural. I kissed my old life goodbye, including Jordan, who was heartbroken. My colleagues gave me a million reasons not to go through with it. They didn't trust the secret society men or think it was safe, but my decision was final, and there was no going back. I said farewell to my friends and entered a med room with a device resembling a hairdryer at a salon.

They placed me on a doctor's table in the seated position and told me to take a deep breath. They assured me it wouldn't hurt and said, "Try not to worry." Right, like that was possible. I was happy, sad, and excited all at the same time. That didn't matter. Once the Scorpio Moon in me makes a decision, that's that.

Manipulated Memories

A nurse put an I.V in my arm and slowly pushed the saline through. I loved the taste in my throat and the tingle down my arm. Then something warm entered my bloodstream, and my muscles relaxed. The substance swirled and rushed like warm water through my veins. Smiling, I laid my head back, and they rolled the machine over. Pulling the device over my head, a white light turned on, and I could feel it pulsating into my skin. A doctor asked me about my job and the secret society tasks I'd completed. Pushing the memories out of my conscious space and into the depths of the subconscious, one at a time. In between, I had thoughts like, "Why am I doing this?" But I silently answered myself, "Freedom from secrecy!" I was determined to enjoy my life, and I couldn't do that when I had to hide everything I was from the world. It felt wrong, and something about the school didn't sit well with me anymore.

The next thing I knew, I woke up in my bed at home, an average teenager. Confused and full of false memories. Thoughts of being a drug user came into my mind, and I wanted a fix. Overnight I was turned into a junkie. Little did I know about the rabbit hole I had just fallen into.

Chapter 5

Heroes aren't born, they are made out of necessity.
~M.J

My new attitude allowed me to enter a dangerous dimension filled with people not afraid to test the boundaries of life itself. Stubborn young kids convinced avoiding life would bring us happiness. Solidifying a sick comradery with everyone experimenting with hardcore drugs. Giving my ego blind courage to push the limits of reality.

People would say I was a noticeably private child clouded by intensity. As my temperament disintegrated, I began wearing heavy makeup and writing dark poetry. When the maverick inside me officially took over, I found myself doing anything to make a statement or throw a middle finger to the man.

Within a year, I fell head over heels for the gangster lifestyle. Raunchy rap and screaming music became my jam and I wore leather coats and combat boots to seem tough. But

Manipulated Memories

I stopped at every mirror or reflection to see if something was out of place. Terrified of not looking my best at every moment.

My dad was busy working as a realtor, and he drank, so I was alone most of the time, and our relationship became awkward once I became a teenager. He seemed bitter towards women after his divorce from my mom. They both talked poorly about each other, but my mom was vicious. She drug his name through the mud and I could tell he didn't appreciate it. So, him dealing with us was probably a reminder of his failed marriage. I don't know if he deserved the things she said, and for a while I didn't know what to think.

While running around the streets I met a girl who took me to a party where I met Dominic. A secretive, sexy, tall, handsome Islander breed that oozed mystery. His thick, dark hair grew past his shoulders in a way mine never could.

He wasn't any better off emotionally, so we acted like it was casual fun, but we talked for hours holding hands when no one was around. It was effortless and I was smitten. I loved that he laughed more than everyone else, a trait we both shared. With a contrasting personality that seemed both optimistic and dramatic, in a person who does crime type of way.

Our sex was primal and ravaging, clawing and panting that seemed to never end. I didn't want to let him go because I wasn't alone with him. I wasn't a troubled teen with no direction, or at least not the only one.

Manipulated Memories

He made me feel like the only person in the room and kissed me longer than necessary no matter who was around. He'd grab my face and first touch my cheek, moving my hair out of the way to softly bite my lips. It was heaven in those moments, peeking my eyes open to see if he was watching me. Smiling when I'd catch a glance of his eyes on mine.

I could feel he wanted to be gentle, but his lifestyle wouldn't allow it. He was wild, almost feral around his friends, and the contradiction was interesting to me. He acted hypocritically possessive and elusive, but people gravitated to him. I couldn't help feeling like a queen sitting on his lap smoking weed with the big kids.

His brother Lenny was my best friend's boyfriend at the time, and he became one of my so-called friends for years. I didn't know that behind the scenes, he was the one convincing Dom to stay away from me, either out of envy or protection. He thought he knew what was best for us, and within a couple months Dominic left me. I was shattered. When Bethan and were Lenny around, I couldn't get away from the reminders of him everywhere. I didn't care what Lenny said nothing would've stopped me from seeing Dom, but that was his brother, and my desires couldn't compete with that.

I didn't tell Dominic I'd fallen in love with him until twenty-one years later. Only after I saw the pattern that I hid my feelings not just from him, but all my relationships. I was terrified of love, real love at least. Yes, I was a kid, but I felt so deeply for others that I was scared it wasn't normal.

Manipulated Memories

Like if I told them, it would weird them out and scare them away. Another example of me feeling like my opinions were harmful. But maybe the universe was saving me from troubles I couldn't see, when Dom texted me his rejection.

By now, my dad didn't know what to do with me, and he must've put together that I was a problem he couldn't fix. Because one day I showed up to our apartment and he was gone, although almost everything he owned had been left there.

I called him from the first cell phone I ever had (which now I'm putting together he probably bought because he had planned to leave me for a while) and asked, "What am I supposed to do, dad?" "You'll figure it out," he responded without mercy. I laughed in confusion. "This is a joke, right?" He explained by saying that he couldn't sell enough houses in our small town and wanted to try to make some money in California. It always came back to money in my family. "You can stay there until the end of the month." My dismay was obvious, but he acted like I'd be fine. I was only seventeen, not old enough to get my own place, and without any money what was I supposed to do?

I did recall he'd mentioned something about being unhappy where we were, but I never dreamt he'd leave me there. I hung up the phone and sat in the living room for hours, calling anyone I could to ask for advice. Lenny and his entourage came over trying to help me understand the situation, but they weren't useful at all. I was gonna have to figure something out on my own.

Manipulated Memories

I stayed in the house as long as I could, going back and forth to my drug-using acquaintances down the street, at least once a day. With no other option, I ended up living with a forty-five-year-old mother of three in a two-bedroom apartment in the slums of town. After we met through our drug connection, even though we had nothing in common except the meth and misery.

Her small apartment was filled with the remains of a four-bedroom home, and more well cared for than you'd think it be. After her three- year-old girl walked in our room with a meth pipe. I had to watch helplessly as she grieved when each child was taken away.

Two teenage boys who sold drugs in the area had become frequent visitors. We'll call them Derek and Jr.

One night there was a "Knock, knock, you home?" from the door and I opened it to what seemed like a regular encounter with the two. When they sat down, I saw looks of fear on their faces. "Did something happen?" They quickly moved their eyes to the ground. "What happened?" I asked again, with no response. "Tell me." Derek pointed at his mouth unable to speak, and Jr. couldn't bring himself to say it out loud without hesitation, "We got in trouble," I barely heard him whisper. "By who?" "No one," he back peddled.

They sat with me in the living room and pulled out a joint, Derek lit and hit it, then passed it to me. I looked down to see the end was covered in blood. "What happened to you?" I passed it back. "You keep it."

Manipulated Memories

The next weekend they both showed up and walked into the house without knocking, Derek smiled big with embarrassment to show me that his jaw had been wired shut.

Since there's a lot of spiritual manipulation happening behind the scenes in this story. People who seem to have no connection are used by satanic means to give messages or cause damage, especially if they're drug users or drinkers. The holes in their magnetic fields allow them to be easily temporarily overtaken by demons with a mission, from a magician. And I don't mean some fairytale creature, but an average person like you or I, who you'd never guess does any kind of magic for a price. The possessed won't understand what's happening and look completely normal to the untrained eye. This is how many got involved in my life without knowing anything about the projects. Let's keep that in mind.

The boys had been told to give me a sedative by someone in town looking for a good time, and after being paid in advance the boys agreed. But spending hours talking with me had changed their minds and they couldn't do it. So Dereks injuries were retaliation for not making good on that deal.

Eventually the lady who owned the apartment became so disheveled and depressed she just stopped coming home, leaving me without a way to pay the bills. Sure, I could've gotten a job, but that thought didn't even cross my mind. I was left with the cluttered mess of her life and forced to give everything she owned to the neighbors.

Manipulated Memories

Each step of my journey was riddled with problems and people screwing me over. I was programmed to believe the world was out to get me, so that's exactly what happened. My intuition told me a hundred times that everything was connected. That these people I surrounded myself with weren't my friends, but the innocence inside me idealized them. I paradoxically understood that they were capable of evil, but my heart couldn't let me believe they'd do it to me.

When I became homeless for the first time, my fear amplified and caused dangerous thoughts to repeat until it consumed me. It scared me so much that I had to turn it off if I was going to survive. I stuffed them into the back of my mind, where they festered. My authentic self-plunged into heavy sadness, and my shadow took over. Now it was me against the world. I decided I hated existing, society, and everyone in it. I became outwardly dramatic from starving for attention while my heart was seething. Always feeling on edge, with no idea why. Calling myself curious, but I was suspicious. Probing inappropriate questions to the people around me and unsure how to interact with kids my age. One step ahead intellectually but ten steps behind emotionally meant I didn't get along with my peers. Honestly, I probably scared them with my dark demeanor and self-hating mannerisms.

My family whispered of one diagnosis or another. "She must be depressed," or "She's probably an anxious child." Although they'd never admit it, my family blamed my mother for being so hard on me. She obviously liked me the least of her kids, hinting I wasn't as good looking as my siblings, and making it obvious by financially spoiling only them.

My relationship with Jera tortured me with neglect. To her, I was the annoying younger sister who wanted to spend every moment with her. Which only pushed her personality farther away, because she craved independence. With an Aries Sun and Moon, she thought of me as pathetic and weak because I couldn't stand up for myself. She didn't understand that I was born that way. I was soft, kind and codependent, nothing like her. Everything I did was wrong, and she was embarrassed to be seen with me. When it came down to it, she and I had long standing karma from past lives. Where I should've been the mean and angry one, but my soft heart couldn't give her the reaction she deserved, and subconsciously she hated me for it.

I had two half siblings who were four and eight years younger, who tried to stand up for me to the alpha women in our lives, but I learned early on that once a scapegoat always a scapegoat. I wasn't like my family, and they had no interest in getting to know me. I felt like a burden just being alive and sometimes I was. Spirits harassed me and most nights I had nightmares with no one to console me.

I want to be clear, I don't believe in identifying people with labels, although it can explain portions of behavior. A title never says everything, and in my opinion, they cause more damage than necessary. With the exploration of neuroscience and psychology without spiritual understandings, we've crippled our society. By labeling ourselves with some harmful defect we hold on tighter to the notion we are broken. Humanity has convinced itself it's at the mercy of dysfunction or illness, a false but brilliant psyop to steal our power. When truthfully, the placebo effect has proven we can heal any dis-ease with the power of our minds.

Which means the opposite is also true. Doctors created illnesses long ago to explain behaviors then made money on false healing through pharmaceuticals, unbeknownst to even themselves. Using gas lighting to convince people of an invisible problem in their mind. When the real culprit for mental suffering is lack of spiritual knowledge. Like that the financial and school systems, alcohol, food, and sexual exploitation are what's actually inducing emotional distress. That then shows up as disease or damage in the body. Over time manifesting in the issues our culture has today.

I'm not suggesting there's no use for such synthetic chemicals but only for a tiny percentage of people actively healing the emotional problem from the root. Without proper healing a dis-ease will not go away, only change form. That's why people have a list of things happening at the same time. One thing can lead to another without proper guidance on how to release it.

I remember growing up that my mind was always in the clouds. Heartbroken by how I saw the world. One day things were okay, and the next, a disaster. Always searching for an unconditional love that didn't exist in the people around me. Yet I knew somehow was out there somewhere. To combat my constant loneliness, I decided the more drugs the better, because they seemed to numb my overwhelming sensitivity. It felt like a way to be different from the kids in school.

In my head, I was a secret agent of the resistance to the systematic principles of a cookie cutter society. Everything about life felt fake to me anyway. Like I was a puppet to an invisible master. I knew life could be more than what I saw, and it bothered me deeply.

I gravitated toward people who felt worse inside than I did. We saw our pain as an excuse to cause as much mischief as possible. Mental conflicts caused me to be ill equipped to deal with emotional anything. So anytime I was confronted with any uncomfortable situation, I dove into a deep depression. After cramming down my feelings for so long, I wondered if I'd ever feel anything. In looking for an escape from who I was and struggling to make sense of life, hostility continued to grow. Until I began channeling my frustrations into poetry and music, which kept me sane when nothing else could. But I will admit that writing this book is the hardest thing I've ever done. A drive for perfection keeps me repeatedly editing without satisfaction. Although I have realized something recently; this isn't a novel. It's my life. As much as I'd love to make it entertaining, my narrative is sad and troubling. In the end, I'll lighten the mood, I promise.

I was mouthy and strong-willed in my ridiculous convictions during these years. Loving towards others but critical of myself. Outwardly rebellious and defiant, but inside I just wanted to fit in. After dropping out of school on the first day of sophomore year, I took a few college classes and got my G.E.D. After hanging around the town my dad left me in for a few months I begged my mom to let me stay with her, although it was the last place on Earth I wanted to be. Not because it wasn't a beautiful house, it was. But the lack of empathy surrounding the women inside rubbed me the wrong way. It felt void of emotions, stale and presumptuous, everything I was not.

By 2003, my mom began bringing up the idea of joining the military. I couldn't help but be suspicious she just wanted to get rid of me. Having left school and no desire for the future meant I had no real excuse to say no. Inside, it hurt that she'd suggest I go into the Army when we were in the middle of a war, but I never said anything. On some level, I wanted to help the nation and be a part of something bigger than myself.

Since my father and stepfather both joined the army young, I believed it was a noble thing to do. But I wasn't exactly excited to join, and the recruiter had to show up unannounced to get me to sign the papers after an all-nighter extasy filled party. I could barely keep my eyes open as the chemicals wore off, while signing my life away on the kitchen table.

Before I planned to leave Jera threw me a going-away party. Twenty people I didn't know showed up at a big house to wish me well and drink. I was an anxious mess about the whole thing and the party was more for Jera than me. Bethan showing up from out of town and Jera getting in a fight definitely made it a night to remember. The house owner told Jera his roommate was gay when we first arrived. I thought that meant he was safe to crash with after I became intoxicated to a not so graceful mess.

I passed out immediately when my head hit the pillow in the blurry room, snuggling the unfamiliar blankets. An unknown male entered the room sometime later, unclothed me from the jeans down and had his way. Pulling my pants almost up to the waist before rolling over and entering dream land, like nothing had happened. It wasn't my first sexual assault, but it was an unlucky continuation of a sad pattern.

Chapter 6

I'm not strange, weird, off, nor crazy, my reality is just different than yours.
~Lewis Caroll

In the middle of that same night, I was awakened suddenly by a weird buzzing sensation, unable to move. My body felt weightless as I began floating upward towards the ceiling. Barely able to keep my eyes open from drowning in alcohol. Disoriented and confused but calmer than expected because something was soothing my energy. A bright light was shining from the ceiling, and I questioned if I'd be crushed to the wall. When I magically flew through the rooftop and up into the stars. It was black outside, but I was focused on the light I'd been drifting towards a couple of hundred yards away.

I couldn't make out the ship behind the light, but I intuitively knew it was there. As I got closer, the feeling of ease increased, and honestly, I had no care in the world. I was slowly lifted through an open door underneath the craft and mechanically set on top a cold metal table. Small machines

Manipulated Memories

automatically clamped my arms and legs down. My eyes began to reveal the three figures of grey beings hovering around me like drones. They had no emotion in their three-foot-tall figures with big heads and small faces. No noses, just holes in the place where they should be. Each with giant black eyes that said nothing.

Behind these three, I saw two taller beings, similar but different. Around five feet tall with long faces and big dark eyes. Another species for sure but an obvious relation. Both had two arms and legs, skinny bodies, and three fingers. It was like watching a cartoon in real life. My mind didn't know what to do with the information, so I ignored that part. Instead, I focused on trying to figure out what they wanted. The larger ones felt mean, angry, and hostile, but that could've been my fear talking.

They began pointing and poking at me when one turned on a machine behind my head. It zipped around and opened a hand-like feature with many needles on it. Moving itself around my body and sticking them into my arm. Without a sound, tears fell down my face as blood poured into the tubes coming off the device, I held my breath until I nearly passed out.

My clothes dematerialized and the table turned me upside down. Probes penetrated me with a hydraulic arm, and a blue goo dripped off the end. I was turned over once again, and the same component probed my back side. The machines ran tests, and a holographic monitor on the side read the results.

Manipulated Memories

Finally, I was cleaned up, dressed, and returned the same way as before.

When this memory came back years later, I would look into who these beings were. The small ones looked like typical Grey's, and the taller ones matched the Maytra, but I wasn't sure. The reptilians I'd seen when I was a kid looked like the Alpha Draconians/Ciakahrr. (Using the names from Elana Danaan's book Alien Races as a reference.)

I woke up the following morning memory wiped, knowing something sexual happened with the gay roommate. Completely mortified, I bailed as quickly as I could. A situation I denied until I went to leave for the Army. Mentally filing it away in the unimportant section of my mind. But I couldn't hide from it when the doctors informed me, I was pregnant, right before I was to get on the plane for basic training. I wasn't ready to have a child and decided that terminating was best.

When I told my mom and sister what happened, they both acted like it was my fault. Saying, "Oh well, you shouldn't have been there." Which taught me to ignore these types of events in the future. My mom said it wasn't a big deal and she would get it 'fixed' as soon as possible. Determined I'd still be going to the Army. Their heartless responses made me question what kind of people they were. But as per usual, I didn't say anything.

The procedure scarred my heart even though I tried to block it out of my mind. But I knew the Source of life existed and loved me no matter my choices. Spirit has since told me that the soul doesn't join the body till its first breath. The child moves around in the stomach only when the soul visits and doesn't stay long. I wish I'd known that then, it would've softened the blow.

Since the military was postponed, I had to get my first job. A classmate of mine had moved to Portland and started stripping, while living with another dancer from the club. It was only an hour away and thinking I could make some good money; I moved into the same apartment and got a job serving drinks at the club. After my dancing try out ended in me crying on stage.

The apartment was rented by a girl named Summer, who'd become my best friend, even though I wasn't hers, for the next twelve years. We had an on again off again friendship with big fights, because she was emotionally unavailable, but I hung on to her coattails whenever she'd let me. I envied her laid back personality and impressive work ethic. She was a baddy before that term ever existed. Our friendship became toxic because we had the same dynamic as me and Jera.

We were both unhealthy, but I loved her. So much so that I would have dated her if she had given me a chance. We made out at parties, but she didn't see me that way when she was sober. I realized I was bisexual then, and it was something I wanted to pursue.

I began to grow into my skin, and even though I wasn't a size two like the other girls, I got better looking every day and didn't know it. Subconsciously, I became competitive, even though I'd never take someone from a friend. This changed the experience I'd have with most women without me understanding why.

We were young, wild, attractive and working hard till four a.m. and playing hard on our days off. Dance clubs and raves in the winter. On fancy boats or looking for big parties when summer came. I struggled to embody the lifestyle and quit the club for what I thought was unfair treatment.

The few months I spent living with the girls in the two-bedroom apartment was like a circus. We had bags on top of makeup boxes inside suitcases on the top of all the shelves. Glitter and hairspray were everywhere. Wine and liquor bottles lined the kitchen sink, and joint roaches and weed leaves covered the coffee table. The communal areas were clean, but the bedrooms were hidden warzones, kept from the public.

Usually at least two of the girls would be fighting, and the other two would be trying to stay out of it. But no matter the drama at home, if there was an event in town, we'd hold our tongues, get dressed up and attend together.

The group consisted of me with longish red hair, the cute short mysterious stoner optimist. My sister Jera who showed off her long blonde hair, blue eyes and beautiful body without shame. The type-a personality and master at getting whatever she wanted. Including when she wanted to move in with us and work at the club. Summer with exotic native skin and long legs who represented the supermodel of the group. And one of my best friends from elementary school who had short blonde and red hair, tall legs, and a fantastic figure. Who's one goal was to have fun no matter the cost.

Everyone but me was showing skin ninety percent of the time. Since we were teenagers and everything was dramatic, I felt left out but never said anything.

One night, friends from the club invited us to a house party, and all four of us headed out to drink. A beautiful female grabbed my face and kissed me aggressively. Her hands groped me as she was clearly intoxicated. She pulled me into the laundry room and hoped for something more. I wasn't willing to have sex with her, and she threw a fit.

As I heard her twin sister looking for her, I announced where she was. When her sister saw me, the other girl grabbed me hard, pulling me towards her saying, "I'm going home with her tonight." "You're not gay!" her sister said. "Yes, I am, and I'm coming out to you right now," she screamed. "I don't believe you," they argued. Jera chimed in with, "Morgan isn't gay either," in a mean tone. "I like girls just as much as guys," I said. She laughed in my face. "You just want attention." I looked at the ground. Knowing I had had a crush on a girl from the club for months. I didn't have the strength back then to challenge her. So I hid my love of women deep inside. It caused me to question myself, something our mother had aroused in me my entire life. I knew in that moment Jera would turn out to be just like her, and there was nothing I could do about it.

Chapter 7

If you hang out with me for too long, I'll brainwash you into believing in yourself and knowing you can achieve anything.

~Unknown

Mid November 2003, I left home for Army basic training, and boot camp felt like a loss of security in my environment. Something I didn't consider until it was gone. The moment I put on that uniform; I was changed forever. My life was no longer about me but about what I could do for the person next to me.

It destroyed the uniqueness of our individualism to create a solid, simple foundation to overlay violence on, brainwashing 101. But at the time, it was empowering. Running four or more miles a day, firing machine guns, and hiking in the woods with a 1920s map and compass. Was ego boosting and crushing at the same time. One moment I had done something I never thought possible and the next I was being made fun of for my last name. There wasn't time to get comfortable with anything. Every day was different and the only thing to look forward to was the off chance that one day you'd get the least vicious drill sergeant available.

We practiced hand to hand battle techniques, and somehow, I came out on top each time. Until then I wasn't aware of my ability to withstand the pressure until I saw a primal internal force push me to do things I never thought possible. It was wild to prove my own belief system wrong in such a short amount of time. I wasn't a weak, helpless victim, I was a soldier now.

One of our last obstacle courses was internally transformative. They wanted me to free jump over a log five feet off the ground. At the end of an all-day obstacle course after crawling with our M-16 through barbed wire fencing and climbing a tower to repel down. Counting how many push-ups and sit ups I did wouldn't be possible.

In front of me was five separate logs, one a little taller than the next. Each jump felt like my muscles were going to collapse, every tendon hurt and screamed for mercy. When I reached the final one, I thought I had nothing left to give. The air produced vapor clouds around my face as I huffed and puffed for air. I knew I was going to hate this. I gathered my strength and pumped myself up in my head. "We got this, everyone else can do it, we can do it."

Once I saw the magnitude of what I was dealing with, an emotional bomb went off in my heart. Tears of pain and exhaustion trickled down my face. I laughed and cried at the same time. The voice changed in my head to "There's no fucking way! I thought it wasn't possible. A joke, right? With contempt, I ran at that stupid log as hard as I could the first five times. I knew the drill sergeants were enjoying my embarrassment, which fueled the fire inside me. My feelings went from shame to anger. I cringed, watching all the guys jump over with no problem. In that moment, I wanted out of the service and off the planet.

My drill sergeant came over smiling, intentionally provoking me. By the eighth attempt, I was the last of over thirty people to go. Dead of winter South Carolina was cold, and everyone wanted to leave. He told me the entire company wouldn't leave until I made it over, no matter how long it took. My heart sank. I tried again and failed, then looked at the sky and asked Source for help.

On the tenth try it felt like a slow mode action scene with everyone watching in suspense. I found myself standing in front of my limitations as a person. That final attempt, when I was at the end of my rope and relying only on the Creator, was a major timestamp in my life.

I threw myself up as hard as I could with one leg higher than the other. The second leg gripped hard on the other side. I shifted my weight in the middle leaning forward with every muscle that had any strength left. And for a moment I didn't know if I would make it. My heart pounded harder than it ever had. My ears rang from the pressure of the squeezing. My back hip didn't want to let go in fear I would hurt myself. But to my disbelief I just barely made it over. People cheered, and power ran through my body like electricity. My Drill

Manipulated Memories

Sergeant and platoon gave me a new level of respect after that.

On another lovely artic day was the dreaded gas chamber. I was the second shortest person in the unit. Which meant me and the shortest girl were always paired together and went first. For this exercise we started with our masks on. After commands from our leaders, we removed them and attempted to say something about how amazing the Army was, our social security number and birthdate. It was nearly impossible, and felt like gasoline ignited my lungs when I breathed the air. Everything inside my throat and nasal cavity came out, gushing down my face, trying to help me remove the gas. My physical trauma alarm had been set off and yet I couldn't leave, it was chaos. Everyone was choking and struggling to inhale. Even when you're prepared for it, it's miserable. Some people ran out screaming in pain, and two girls behind us panicked so bad they had to try three separate times.

My battle buddy had a hard time handling the poison in her face and was frantic to get out. I made the mistake of following her too close. She started to yell, wailing her arms with her bulletproof helmet in hand around like a handkerchief. Blinded by the gas in my eyes, I didn't see to protect my face. My upper lip met her helmet dead center in the middle of her swing.

It was the first time I had to surrender to the universe and be introduced to Source's sense of humor. It forced me to understand that no matter how much something sucks (and that did), it could always get worse. There was an instant need to see the brighter side even here. Appreciating the laughter, I would have about it later.

Since I was training during the Christmas holiday, I got a break in the middle. For two weeks they sent me home to my bougie family. But the brainwashing had already set in, and I looked at them like they were peasants. Civilians we called them, a lower life form. People who needed to be protected.

They praised my new muscular body and yet I still wasn't comfortable in it. My mom Judy sat on the couch petting her expensive cat, "Better watch out Jera, she'll kill you with her pinky." Everyone laughed and I rolled my eyes. Feeling blank and still bitter that she could care less I might die in battle. That, that would make her proud. I could feel that I was respected by her in this moment. And the rebel inside me wanted to flip her off. I smiled and watched her facial expressions for longer than necessary. Speculating what life story could create a woman like her.

My eyes scanned her entire house in slow motion. Not one picture of her three kids anywhere. A beautiful Christmas tree with silver and gold furnishings, but no child made ornaments, although we had made them. I had brought pictures of my training home and knew they would never see the light of day. None of this was something to fuss about now but someday I wouldn't be able to ignore it anymore. Who was I raised by, and how did she become that person?

When I got back to base, I continued writing music and poetry, because it helped calm the pressure in my mind. And

Manipulated Memories

sometimes after our hurry-up and wait training day, thirty people would listen as I sang "Silent Night" or the latest Lauren Hill, on the stairwell in between our barracks. I felt compelled to soften the mood but wasn't sure where that feeling came from.

In the sleeping bay of forty bolted to the ground steel bunk beds were young girls heartbroken with homesickness. We would cry, laugh, and make fun of ourselves to combat the eerie quiet of the cement surroundings. I noticed we were all strong women in teenage bodies looking to find ourselves. Painfully aware we were trying to make it through a male dominated environment. Holding onto our hopes and dreams of the future for dear life. Looking for the respect of our families, terrified we would fail to meet their expectations.

Dropping out wasn't an option, although every day, I wanted to. I cried rivers of tears all the time; we all did. And at the end of each night, we'd go into our bunks, put the blankets over our heads and quietly scream. Every morning was torturous after only four hours of sleep, and we sometimes dragged each other out of bed. Every day the desire to fit in kept me going. Constantly paranoid people would think of me as weak.

All I could do was create a tough exterior, when inside, I just wanted to make it through. Being a woman meant I worked twice as hard, as the physical challenges and emotional beratement felt intended for my failure. I didn't complain, but I did notice.

Manipulated Memories

To help us feel better, we kept pictures in our lockers of our families as motivation. But we were so called troubled kids with challenging backgrounds and self-esteem issues due to abuse at home. Personalities that didn't match our family structure, so we were ostracized. It turned us into at risk kids who would more likely see jails and institutions than a typical career. So, there we were, sent, or deciding on our own to become the shield of our country.

Sometimes I think about why killing each other even became a thing on this planet. I know it's a deep topic most people don't like to think about, but that's because brainwashing runs deep.

Each day, a new assessment of willpower, patience, strength, and cunning. Simultaneously studying diplomacy and assertiveness, looking at a situation from all angles to get an advantage over the enemy. We saw how each step in this process highlighted strengths and weaknesses we never knew we had. For the first time, I saw the struggle from other people's points of view. The deep connection between us in this insanity created a foundation for bonding. Responsible for the camaraderie of soldiers everywhere.

I found myself leaning toward becoming a leader. Not because I was more capable since I was only one tiny link in the chain, but because my creativity inspired them. I was convinced not to let them break my spirit, which inspired others to do the same. Acting like an adult for the first time created a positive ripple in the world that I didn't need to see to believe.

Manipulated Memories

On our last day, I woke up one minute before our human alarm, knowing it was our last ruck march. A drill sergeant walked into our bay and yelled. "Get up maggots, you've got ten minutes to be downstairs for breakfast."

I saw that Private Powell was still in bed after I brushed my teeth, covered in her blankets. I tapped her gently and reminded her to get up. "Leave me alone, I'm not coming!" She snapped at me, but I couldn't let her quit. "Listen, Powell, you can do this." She slammed the blankets down with both arms, poking her head up in a tizzy. "Fine, fuck!" I smiled and related deeply to her sentiment. "You're preaching to the choir," I uttered with a grin under my breath. I waited for her to stumble out of bed and grab her uniform. Watching the markings her face made as she couldn't hide her misery.

Each of us walked into the chow hall hoping to get enough to fill our stomachs. But my food insecurities made the area feel loud and hostile, I squirmed in discomfort. I wasn't my normal extra pounds body type anymore, but I still felt like I was. And I never got used to eating in front of that many people. Every moment seemed amplified, and my nervous system was on edge.

One long table with a row of servers behind it handed out low-grade cafeteria foods, with only a yes or no. Like everyone else, I said yes to everything, knowing that I needed my strength for the day. Preferences didn't matter anymore, and pleasure had no place there. I shoveled as much as possible down my throat as quickly as I could. While hearing

Manipulated Memories

personal jabs from the drill sergeants from all directions. "Are you sure you want to eat that fatty?" "Hurry up, we don't have all day." "I'm getting bored, let's go!"

Although I knew the meanness was contrived, it bothered me. I looked at them like they were aliens. Who the heck would want that job? And how do they just turn it off when they go home? "I bet some of them don't... ugh," I thought. During my stay I saw a few break character a couple times and it helped me get through. To believe people were that awful wasn't something I was ready to understand.

We gathered in the center of the company. At least sixty people stood nervously waiting for instructions. The cold air made our breath create small puffy clouds dance around us. Our silent shivering was masked by anticipation.

Each soldier lined up in their respective platoons and walked to the building to gather and fit the rucksacks. The apprehension caused our minds to race, and dread to build. It was quiet but the energy was blaring.

"The track is over twenty miles." A drill sergeant lied to stress us out. The blood drained from my face, and I giggled with fear. Knowing it would be with a weighted rucksack crushing my shoulder blades and pushing me into the ground, through the winter snow. No matter how long it really was, it was gonna suck. "This will be the hardest thing you've ever done, and it's supposed to be. Stay in a single file line, shortest to tallest. There will be no talking or whining while I'm in charge, you can cry later."

Manipulated Memories

One by one we made our way out of the training area and into the wide-open hills. As we began, I noted that as I expelled my much-needed body heat, I felt an awkward tingle and un-scratchable itch. After failing to find comfort, I succumbed to the torture. Unable to rationalize the situation, the world got hazy.

My mobility went into autopilot, and I looked like the living dead. Blisters on both feet appeared within the first few miles and the raw flesh stuck to my socks, covered in blood and sweat. The leather rubbed back and forth over the open wounds, causing a pain I cannot describe here. The whole time I was thinking to myself, "This is the dumbest thing that's ever existed." While my tiny legs were shuffling and barely making it a foot at a time. To get through it, I was forced to cheerlead for myself as much as humanly possible. "I'm almost done with this whole thing; can't fall out now. I can do this. If the boys can do it, I can do it. Long legged, bigger lunged fuckers."

It was a nightmare. One hour after the next with deafening silence. As the sun was going down, I saw what looked like the base in front of us, and scolded the sky, "That better not be a mirage, or I might actually die."

The entire company slowly limped into the outdoor headquarters. Forcing each step now, I began chuckling, ranting, cursing, and wanting to die. So close now and yet still doubting that I could finish it. As we made it back, I was nearly screaming in pain. Trudging into the main training area, we found the entire complex engulfed in the music of

Manipulated Memories

"We Are the Champions," by Queen. The sound vibrated off the walls in such a way that every cell in my body was on fire. Finally, months of tears, entire body muscle aches, and psychological warfare were over.

I didn't know it, but I had elevated to a new level of existence at that moment. After a short debrief, we were allowed to call our families. And the power of that phone call was like a tidal wave that had me barely able to speak, because I was overflowing with joy and pride in who I was. It was arguably the best feeling I'd ever had, vulnerable and yet unbreakable.

Shortly after, I was moved to another base for A.I.T (job school) in Augusta, Georgia. Because, when I joined, I was allowed to pick any job I wanted based on my test scores. I chose to be a networking specialist called 74B, which later changed to 25B, part of the Signal Command, which trained at Fort Gordon. I was taught to set up computer networks from the ground up, a cushy job as far as the Army goes. We started with a course on Cisco networking systems six days a week, twelve hours a day for three months straight. We worked hard all day and enjoyed our warm nights with sweet tea and conversation.

I soon dated a wonderful man from my unit named Aiden who thought he wanted to marry me after only two months. A kind soul with a southern accent that had me talking that way for a while. I met his family, and they were precious. A rowdy fun loving, wholesome type of crowd. Except they ate boiled peanuts, gross! We never once fought, although I had

Manipulated Memories

a crush on someone else when we met. I was honest about the situation, and he handled it well. He was tall with dark features, handsome, and always smiling. A big guy with a gentle spirit and really cute butt.

Our company lived together in small apartment type rooms with ten or so on each level. During the day we studied our jobs and learned how to be full-time soldiers. They allowed us to stay out overnight on the weekends, and like the other soldiers before us, we rented out entire hotels to stay up and party.

Right before I was done with school I got pulled out of my orders for Germany and "hand-picked" to be part of a Stryker brigade. A higher performing tactical team with the latest equipment the Army (or so they say) had at the time. This seemed sketchy to me, but I couldn't do anything about it. I didn't want to go home; I wanted to go anywhere else. But they wanted me close to the project's headquarters. Aiden got sent to airborne school at Fort Bragg, and that was the end of that.

I went into my regular Army unit and moved home to Fort Lewis, Washington. Where I would experience an unprecedented level of persecution because of that agreement.

In the background of my story, the boys I had mentioned before, Damien and Jordan, had grown up being manually set up to destroy us all. With hypnotic suggestions and poor teaching about women, they had no way of knowing what they'd become. The anger they were programmed to have fed into their minds and grew with time. Damien wasn't part of the initial problem and only trained with us a few times, because he was traveling with his family out of the country. But he had fallen into infatuation with me from a desire for older women. The leaders saw that and used it to their advantage.

Since the Stryker Brigade was new, we found out once we got to our barracks that we had to get the old, dilapidated building up and running. After it sat for who knows how many years. And during the process I spotted an adorable baby face blonde boy in my new company. He smiled at me sheepishly and I could tell he was a quiet one. I loved the idea of ruining that about him. I thought it was better for people to be outspoken and unapologetic at that age. But he was sheltered and as innocent as they come, something I didn't relate to at all. We were from opposite backgrounds, and he had plans for the future that I didn't even understand. His brain was the sexiest thing I'd ever been introduced to at that juncture in my life. Our young love started quickly and codependently attached intensely. He was good to me and smart and dependable and sincere and I didn't know what to do with it. I only knew chaos and disfunction. His loving nature and aspirational outlook on life gagged my cynicism. I tried my best to smile and work harder than I wanted to, to impress him. But he was a special type of overachiever, the kind that woke up at four in the morning to go work out before we did physical training. Then chose to go to college after working twelve hours. I felt uneasy in the relationship because I didn't feel good enough for him.

After being in Washington for around a year I got tasked to be the assistant to the First Sergeant running the company. Which had me forced to do mediocre tasks like get him coffee or clean the already cleaned areas. I was bored out of my mind for twelve hours every day. Until he asked me to help him set up and change the slides for his training meetings with the company leaders.

The Commander, XO, and other higher-ranking members would meet once a week and discuss how we'd proceed. The way I saw it was, at least I got to see what we were doing before it happened. I'm sure the boys didn't appreciate my new first sergeant's pet status. Which was most likely due to a tighter than necessary uniform I used to feel somewhat female, in the sea of green. Either way, being one of three and at most four girls in the unit meant I stood out, whether I wanted to or not.

On a random day in autumn my life changed forever. I was taken into an office and told someone wanted to see me. I stood at the parade rest and waited, irritated that I didn't know what was going on. When an older gentleman I didn't recognize as one of the base leaders walked in. He asked about my job and my computer skills, then smiled at my response. And out of the blue, like it was nothing, offered me a new position in the Air Force on what he called a twenty and back program. A mission into outer space. I didn't even ask about the details, just jumped at the chance immediately without hesitation.

He proposed that I consider a few stipulations, and to myself I whispered, "Always a catch." He explained how I couldn't ever tell anyone I went or had anything to do with the Space Force. He left out the bigger details, but by then, I was used to the military's games. They could've told me I'd have to shave my head and learn to walk on my hands, and I'd been happy too. No one could've talked me out of that opportunity. I was convinced it was the best thing that could ever happen, and on some level, it was.

Chapter 8

All civilizations become either spacefaring or extinct.
~Carl Sagan

Since it was a secret, it was easy to agree and go without all the paperwork usually done in switching branches. I didn't know at the time that it would only be the first of two enlistments. Before I left, it was explained to me that time isn't the same in space. They assured me they'd bring me back into my life twenty years later, and no one would ever know. Once again, I agreed to remove my memories when I returned. A pattern that kept showing up, whether I knew it or not.

First, I was assigned to a four-duty station contract. Alpha Centauri Outpost 347, then Venus, Mars, and Saturn. I'd have smaller assignments along the way that weren't specified in the contract, which was typical for the military. And they were more than happy to have Mia 369 on the Force.

Manipulated Memories

A small group of us including my boyfriend Alex, were taken to the McChord Air force base and shuttled to a hidden underground terminal. Then escorted onto a fighter jet shaped craft with multiple colors of dark grey, made out of an alien material that shined like glass. Filled with technologies I'd never seen. The inside was oval, and the seats surrounded the outer circumference in a perfect circle. In the middle was a shiny platform with holographic images of the flight details. That reminded me of the movie Total Recall, where the monitor doubled as a control panel. Everywhere I looked, metal rounded finishing's melded into the interior.

When we belted into the seats, the straps pulled down over our torsos like a racecar, and the engine purred like a cat as we took off. A soft buzzing came from the machines and excitement kept a smile on my face. Our group looked at each other in amazement and disbelief. Although we couldn't see it, we could feel the ship prepare to hyperjump. A slight tension built, and a small force pulled us backwards for a millisecond before blasting us forward through time itself. In a flash we went from inside the Earth's gravity to a section of space that wasn't in the grip of it.

As we left Earth's atmosphere the buckles around our torsos automatically unlocked and retracted into the seats. Over an intercom that reached the entire ship was an announcement that we were free to move around during the overnight flight. I quickly got up and inspected the ship. In complete awe of the spectacular view of space through the windows. Blackness I didn't know could exist surrounded us;

pop marked with sparse luminous dots that mesmerized my eyes. I wondered who'd I meet out there. What I'd see now that I had no Earthly limitation. The feeling of freedom was overwhelming and frightening. I smirked when I thought about ending up on some remote planet with a new culture. Maybe they'd take me in, and I'd leave Earth behind forever. There was always a part of me trying to run from who I was there. Mia wanted to get away from the government's control, but she didn't know how to get that across. So, she kept a feeling of fear within me, a suggestion to run away. It was the best she could do from her position, to help me survive the future. Adventure for us was the one thing we couldn't be promised. A calm, healthy, normal life. Something we wouldn't see for a while.

The child within me jumped up and down with joy about our new venture. But I was still nervous of the unknown, even if I couldn't admit it. I had seen the movies like everyone else, and what if some of them were true. Did I just make the best or worst decision of my life?

The ship stopped at the moon for three days to get our assignments and uniforms. Where after a briefing, I was pulled aside to have an intense conversation with a female commander. Her office was filled with awards and recommendations that hung on the walls. I knew she must've done something big to have such medals. We greeted with small talk before she hit me with, "I don't think you understand what could happen up here?" She paused, looking down. "What do you mean?" I asked confused. "Sweetheart you need to keep close to people you can trust. Some men you'll encounter haven't even seen a woman in years, and the longer you're up here, the more chances you'll run into one." I knew what she meant but I hadn't thought about it. She opened her desk and pulled out a collapsible electric baton and signed it out to me to use. Making sure I knew I had to give it back. Leaving me with, "This will stun any man to the ground no matter how big he is, don't lose it." This scared me tremendously, but I was already in and denied any real danger.

We talked about my qualifications, and she told me her plan to support my enlistment by sending me and Alex to officer school. She asked me to think about what I'd like to study and gave me a day to figure it out. I thought about my different interests like cosmology and art. But in the end, I knew I wanted to understand people because they fascinated me. And I thought I could relate to them better if I understood how their minds worked. She agreed that my choice was suitable, and I could benefit the service by improving morale between races. Which at the time sounded intimidating but I convinced myself I was up for the challenge.

I realized later that she wanted me to be protected by my rank. Which I would learn was pretty much the only chance a human female had to make it without incident, if they were lucky.

So off I went to a school on a small planet in Alpha Centauri where I was one of only two women in the course.

Manipulated Memories

Touching down on the planet's surface I saw a landscape of soft milled orange dust. With rounded hilltops and mountains, and magnificent purple skies. Its two suns blasted hot all day, and the smaller one was visible at night as the brightest star I'd ever seen. Vegetation was scarce with a few blue trees and scrawny bushes but not much else. The view was breathtaking to a single worlder like myself.

Class took place inside a giant copper squared building filled with over three hundred people from all over the galaxy. I would study for five years taking classes about other species and learning to be an officer. Choosing to study psychology was profoundly eye-opening. When learning things about the mind hidden from the textbooks on Earth. The truths about the connection to our bodies and how each nerve connects to a chakra. It blew my mind with facts that opened my understanding of energy.

My favorite teacher was a non-human female named Sierra. She taught spirituality and demonstrated extraordinary gifts like clairvoyance, (seeing etheric energy), Claircognizance (knowing information instantly), and many others. Her skills were mysterious and otherworldly. She taught us automatic writing and ways to mentally protect ourselves.

From the moment we met, I was infatuated and craved to be alone with her. And although I had a boyfriend, I daydreamed of us together and became distracted. I tried to stop myself, but I was helpless to the electricity that showed up when she entered the room. Her slim build, curly blonde hair, and blue eyes were enchanting. She stood at least three inches shorter than me, and her big presence didn't match her size. Her pointy ears reminded me of the elvish in the Lord of the Rings. There was something about her that had my heart, and I'd have to hide it for the next four years.

The things she taught us helped me get through my troubles when the men were malicious because they didn't want me around. But I stuck it out and became an honor student.

Sierra slipped a note into my hand during my graduation ceremony as I walked across the stage. The anticipation had me sneaking into the hallway to open it. "Meet me in the science lab when this is over," it said. I hurried there as soon as I could, my heart pounding. When she opened the door, there was a look on her face I'd never seen before. She walked towards me in a less than innocent manner, not saying a word. She grabbed my chin and kissed me aggressively. Surges of energy pulsated throughout my body, and it was clear something was magnetizing us.

Enthralled in that moment, we began to undress when someone opened the door. Her face turned red, and we both started to laugh. I looked at her confused, and she put her hand to my face. "I know you love your boyfriend, but he has a secret he needs to tell you, or I will."

I practically floated back to my room unable to stop smiling, where my long-term boyfriend Alex waited for me. I informed him of what Sierra had done and said, and he sat down, slouching his shoulders and crossing his hands on his head. Then replayed his atrocities. Admitting that he had an affair with my younger sister back on Earth. Telling me they'd slept together six times and regretted it terribly. That was all the excuse I needed to be done with him forever. He knew he'd crossed a line you can't come back from.

Luckily for me Sierra was there to soften the blow, and although I was hurt, I was excited to see where it would go. It wouldn't be easy to spend time with her. Student teacher relationships were a no go, and I didn't want her to get fired. She was a sweet, gentle soul who didn't want to break the rules, but neither of us could refuse the intensity of our connection. We became best friends and hid our sexual relationship.

Early on I learned things about her that took my breath away. Like that she was royalty in her culture, and soon to be forced into an arranged marriage. Which broke my heart and caused me to contemplate a million ways for us to stay together. We even planned to steal a spaceship and run off into the stars. But something magical happened when our base's command asked for volunteers on a classified mission, at exactly the right time.

Before we left, we were told it was on a base called Cortus and that it'd be a risky job because the technology we'd be using could be unpredictable. They didn't hesitate when saying we weren't guaranteed to return. When we got on site, our new commander briefed us about working with a stargate to look for new planets that could support life. Allowing us to travel far distances in the blink of an eye. It was a manufactured portal that connected to the naturally occurring ones all over the galaxy (yes, including on Earth). I felt like I was in a dream, I had seen the shows about this sort of thing, and I wasn't thrilled. This was dangerous and there was no way around it. Sierra and I looked at each other nervously, and I could tell she was pissed, but we were already in and there wasn't anything anyone could do now. Unless she wanted to leave me, which for now was out of the question. I tried to console her, but she didn't speak to me for days.

Sierra's job was to use her gifts to plan the explorations, because our instruments could only guess what kind of climate and foliage were there. Her visions would give us the most likely potential dangers. But since they're multiple dimensions of time, nothing she saw was set in stone.

The base itself was a small round matte black disc suspended in space. With only ten rooms available around the outside for personnel. In the middle was a vast room that housed the stargate. A twenty-foot-tall circular interdimensional man-made artifact. That looked like a thin pool of water suspended in midair, but it was filled with a type of plasma surrounded by a horseshoe of stone, inscribed with a sacred language. That only two people on board could read or know how to use.

Once a month, me, Sierra and another male soldier would suit up in navy blue jumpsuits, (made of a miracle fabric that could withstand a nuclear attack) and our issued helmets that displayed holographic depictions of our physical condition and environment on the face shield, to explore the galaxy.

Sierra would astral travel to the potential portal and bring back as much data as possible. Which we learned right away wasn't exactly the same as the physical world. We knew even the minor differences could mean someone's life if we weren't careful. The continual stress took a toll on everyone, especially her. We were three young soldiers asked to discover new worlds. A depth of responsibility that sat heavily on our hearts. You could cut the tension with a knife before every mission, and we grew to dread our job.

Each of us took hovering vehicles called buggies, with anti-gravity propulsion systems. The biggest one (the size of an S.U.V) was assigned to our male counterpart, equipped with an arsenal for fighting in case we needed it. Mine was bulky and stored cargo and supplies. Sierras looked like a tiny tank with wheels that could turn into propellers to be used underwater.

Most places we went were desolate uninhabitable worlds, with super-hot or too cold atmospheres that we didn't last more than five minutes on. A few had potential until we found organisms that would eat your skin or water that would kill you. We lost two male counterparts, one to a storm and one to an animal we couldn't have predicted would be there. And those events were soul changing. I learned just how lucky we are here. Earth is heaven compared to what's out there, and we should respect that.

Manipulated Memories

On one of our days off, Sierra and I sat cross legged in the middle of our room inside a ring of holographic candles. I could tell she was hiding something, but I didn't want to pry. In silence, she took both my hands in hers. I looked up to see her beautiful blue eyes tearing up.

She looked at me and said, "I've gotten permission to help you." "What do you mean?" A tear rolled down her chin as she smiled. "There's a lot I haven't told you about your future. You wouldn't want to know right now. It wouldn't change anything." I shook my head, muttering that that wasn't possible. She nodded without agreement and lowered her head, "You won't remember any of this, but I've found a way to keep you safe. I've asked the Source to activate your psychic gifts early. To make sure you make it." "What do you mean I make it?" "There's a lot you don't know about who you are, and in the future, you will be met with that knowledge." "I don't understand," I whispered frustrated. She calmly continued, "I know, and that's okay. Listen, you are stronger than you give yourself credit, and I'd put money on you for sure, but I'm going to activate your gifts, so you have a better chance." "You're freaking me out," I gasped. "It means, when you are ready for the truth, it will appear to you. You will see your entire life's history and future, then you'll know what to do and when to do it. It'll happen when you're truly okay with yourself, because everything you've been through is for a reason and has nothing to do with who you are. You'll be a superhero one day, and if I can help that become a reality, I'm honored too. So close your eyes, feel your heartbeat, and listen to your breathing." I humored her although I was less than happy about it. A loud 'pop' sounded in my ears. I felt something electric enter my forehead, and a burning sensation followed. She whispered, "Don't move." Every cell in my body lit on fire, and my eyes began watering tears. I could feel an energy vortex in my heart spinning, and something was opening and igniting. I thought I saw an angel with full gold and white wings smiling, and in a flash it was over.

When I opened my eyes, it was like seeing the world for the first time. New colors swirled around me, shiny, sparkly hues surrounded everything, as if magic colored dust was radiating off matter itself. I was beaming with joy and undoubtedly the happiest I'd ever been. I lifted Sierra's bowed head with my fingers, softly saying, "I could never forget you," kissing her deeply. Even though this was the most miraculous moment of my life. This experience had to be our secret.

After another non successful yet extremely stressful mission, we got a visitor to the station. This time, a giant reptilian without wings showed up to check our progress. He sauntered slowly around our quarters with his ten-foot-tall muscular rigid body, probing for information about our findings. Demanding to know if there was something we weren't telling him. The intensity in his voice was intimidating when he spoke to us like ants. We stood quietly while he bent eye to eye with the man running the gate.

Manipulated Memories

In secret, everyone in the Force talked about the reptilian's desire for control, but this was the first time it was shoved in my face. As much as I wanted to believe that we were in charge of ourselves, the evidence was in. There wasn't anything farther from the truth.

I was promoted to 1st Lieutenant after only a year on Cortus because my superiors recognized the level of danger, I made it through and let me know I was lucky to be alive. I earned my stripes faster than most, and it'd ruffle some feathers. We held a small ceremony to change my insignia, and I was honored by the crew with words of empowerment. I knew my fellow colleagues would be jealous, but you don't say no to a new rank.

This started a longstanding feud with anyone whom I trained with. The stargate team was so classified I couldn't tell them the truth. So, they made jokes and said I was sleeping around. As a female in the military, you learn to live with the egos of young men without taking it personally.

That was the only time in the year I was there when someone outside our group came to the ship until just before our contract was up. Sierra's family sent an envoy requesting her to go home, clearly unhappy with her current relationship. They side-eyed me without shame. And although it wasn't a sexual orientation problem, it was a bloodline faux pas. They pointed out the flaws of the human race one by one. The destruction and violence we were known for and the fact that we were considered infants in the bigger picture. Children who don't know how to get along, easily swayed into selfish acts. I couldn't argue such a true statement, but Sierra tried to.

She didn't want to leave me, and it was up to us to find another place to go. Since we had such high-security clearances, I could look into other high-level projects. After some digging around, I found another secret mission, this time on Venus. To work security with a botanist on healing serums for the sick. It sounded like a dream come true, and we packed our bags, heading to what people call the wishing well, the most advantageous place in the solar system. Jumping on a large cargo ship with genuine excitement for the first time, happy to get away from the misogyny of the military.

Chapter 9

The whole world is a school of virtue.
~ Manly Hall/Socrates

The lifeforms on Venus were only found in higher vibrational dimensions than our natural state. And to get there, we first had to be dropped on the planet in the middle of nowhere. Where it was hot, desolate and swirling with dust. We suited up in high-tech helmets and body suits to manage the harsh climate and made our way onto the hangar. Each of us were handed small round silver metal devices as we got closer to the target. Through the wind of the open door, we were told to stick it to our chest plate and push the center button. It activated silently and created a transparent bubble shield around us.

Five of us jumped one at a time, our legs dangling as we hovered down. Each landing and running toward a pyramid shaped building on a walkway etched in the ground pointing south, as fast as we could in a single file line. A shimmering halo of light got brighter as we approached the end of the markings.

Manipulated Memories

We entered the unmarked building cautiously, and each person's name was greeted as we passed through the door. We cautiously followed the markings on the floor. Gasping at the beautiful surroundings that contrasted the building's plain exterior. Brilliant gold markings covered the walls in circular patterns from ground to ceiling. With symbols and languages, I'd never seen. The space was empty, but the security was obvious.

Our faces were illuminated by the gold diffracted light circling the structure in the middle. As we got closer to the light, we could see that the entire building was woven around that area. The markings all stretched towards the center. Where a five-foot-tall triangular energetic doorway had ripped a hole in space/time. To my human eyes, it looked two dimensional. Like reality had been cutout with a stencil.

They ordered us to duck our heads and walk in one at a time. My skin buzzed with electricity, like soft lightning dancing on the skin, as I stepped through. The entire building grew in size, and I was standing in the middle of a military base crowded with people. I gawked at the surroundings as my mind tried to register that an inconspicuous shack in the middle of the desert turned into a high tech supercity in seconds.

Intuitively I knew my body had changed but I didn't know exactly how. In time, I learned that the density was different from Earth. That my body was now less heavy and soft to the touch, bouncy and less rigid than before.

Manipulated Memories

The Venetian city was magical, and it didn't disappoint. The world was decorated with singing waterfalls and giant living pools, where people floated with ribbons and hoops. Bright iridescent colors lined the streets and joy-filled the space. It was lighthearted and loving, without a trace of darkness anywhere. The wildlife was docile and unafraid of the other beings, and the trees could talk telepathically.

I was briefed about helping the scientists on the base that sat on the top of a mountain on the outskirts of the city. Its triangular shape shined holographic colors throughout the region from its glass-like substance. I was intrigued when they told me the workers floated up and down pressurized tubes on each level to travel the complex. The building itself was magnificent, and the technology reminded me of the Capitol in the Star Wars movies.

The citizens' homes were built a few inches to a few feet off the ground, so as to not disturb the fauna. The walkways were platforms that glowed from underneath, held by small strong pegs. The houses coexisted with the trees and rocks as supports, and the respect for the planet was evident. Councils of residents oversaw different sections of 'governmental' tasks, and the people were continually involved in the workings of their society.

Children were born from anyone and taken to a part of the planet specifically created for child rearing. This lessened the guilt or remorse parents could experience if they didn't have a parental urge. And allow those who couldn't have babies, a way to support the culture. People only worked where they felt inspired and if they wanted to, which most of them did. If someone called in or wasn't feeling well, someone would go to their home and work through their issues. It wasn't a utopia like you may be thinking. It was a well-organized mega community that learned its methods through spiritual elevation. It sought to grow and thus it did.

It was filled with beings of all types, but I worked with a group of blue skinned, pointy chin Arcturians in a science lab. Their feminine energy oozed importance and intelligence. Wisdom poured off their auras, and I felt safe in their presence. Most had gold tribal tattoos covering their entire body, just like the markings around the doorway. They exuded patience and diligence with permanent genuine smiles. So divinely connected you knew everything they said was coming straight from the Source of life itself. So powerful no one questioned their motives, because they'd ascended to a level of mastery famously revered throughout all existence.

My job was to support them when looking for new substances to treat diseases, in areas that could be dangerous. But over time, it became diluted by my regulations. We wanted to do more studies but were held back by the procedures and requirements. First, they wouldn't let us test new products. Then I was refused permission to help them in the field. It was like they didn't want me to do my job. My anger motivated me to sign a grievance to their superiors, which didn't sit well with my commanders.

Either way, I was promoted to Captain after three years. Then I became the head of a complaint department. That helped women who had been sexually harassed, and I started to get a name for being a troublemaker.

Sierra and I lived together, and one day, she asked me to stand with her while she commanded the wall to produce a full-length mirror. Opening her bag, she pulled out a belt with a funny buckle, and I waited as she turned it on. A screen popped up in front of us with a menu. She scrolled through and picked an option. I giggled in shock when her hair turned silver and her eyes green. She picked another option, green skin and white eyes, and we played around cycling through the different choices.

We figured out only superficial modifications were possible, because it wouldn't alter her shape or proportions, or she would've made herself taller, I know it. She did cat eyes and added a tale. Then asked what I wanted to see, and I gave her suggestions. Blue hair and black eyes, then yellow hair and big lips. We laughed for hours, changing her nails to be super long and her eyebrows blonde. Bonding for hours on the possibilities that were endless.

The one-night Sierra was working an overnight shift, I woke up unable to move after going to bed. Looking at a ten-foot-tall Mantis being, hovering over me with a vile looking menacing. Speaking to me telepathically, he whispered in monotone, "You are relaxed, calm, and sleepy. You don't see anything. This is a dream. It's safe to go back to sleep child." In front of him was a large needle that he stuck into my stomach. Guiding the plunger with telekinesis, he pushed the serum into my womb. His power was impossible to fight, and

Manipulated Memories

I fell asleep. But when I woke up, I knew something was wrong and told my leaders to check the security tapes. He was caught on camera coming into my room, detained, and tried for breach of procedure. I was surprised they'd go to such lengths. I had the eggs removed and was forced to change duty stations right away, but Sierra wasn't allowed to come with me.

During our last night together, I suggested we relax in the self-heating bathtub. A concept I knew she hadn't experienced before, which I thought was ridiculous. She laughed at me because of my excitement. I filled it with roses and bubbles that smelled like vanilla. When she got in, she had a sad look that I could hardly bear. I wanted to comfort her heart and let her know she was the best thing that had happened to me so far in this life. So, I began and she followed listing our favorite parts of each other, with nonstop tears pouring down our faces in admiration.

"I love how your hair curls over your temples and sits complimenting your face."

"I love how you design dinner each night, as it's a show to remember."

"I love it when the light hits your face in the morning and sparkles off your skin."

"And I love your optimism each day, even in the face of adversity."

"I love how strong you stand, like a nine-foot-tall beast in a tiny body."

"I love how you think of me before yourself always."

"I love how I'll never forget you as long as I live." That one crushed me.

"I love the idea that someday I'll remember you again and it'll be like the first time we met." I lied.

"I love how you know what to say to cheer me up."

"I love how the infinite sits inside you, and you act like it's normal."

We laughed and made love for the final time. More passionate and sensual than ever before and I felt a closure to us that I didn't expect. There couldn't have been a better ending to something so special.

The next morning, we kissed until the very last moment, and I didn't care that I could taste the saltiness of her tears. It felt unfair and cruel to have to leave her. A crew member with tears in his eyes had to physically pull us away from each other. Since I was the last to get on the cargo ship headed for my next duty station. In that last heavy moment, we both knew we would never see each other again. She would marry, and I'd have my memories blocked, and for a while, this otherworldly love would be erased from my life.

In a contrasting move I made my way to Mars Max. A harsh compound in the center of the almost dead planet. Our ship entered through a small deep tunnel, because it was cold, dusty, and only bearable underground.

Underneath the crust was dense with red and brown-colored stones similar to Utah's landscapes, as far as the eye

Manipulated Memories

could see. But inside was decorated with immense caverns used to create small cities. Civilian homes were dug out of the surrounding rock. Money was scarce there, and most people lived in poverty, lining the streets begging.

Creatures of all kinds walked the alleys, and giant eight legged spiders lived on the manmade mountains. I didn't expect they'd be agreeable and curious. Others were puffy, round, gelatinous beings with small arms and legs. Some were hairy, some were tall, some had small heads and others big noses. It was fascinating to be surrounded by such species diversity.

A mix of military and civilian robots littered the open spaces and left a hue of sadness. Without resources the residents couldn't leave, and you could tell they wanted to. The military's job was to keep the peace in the city. But when that many people are miserable, it's nearly impossible to police. On base was the cleanest area for hundreds of miles, and I felt lucky just to have a nice place to sleep. There were very few usable pools of water in our area. Which gave few bathing options and left the water green and undrinkable without processing.

I've heard a rumor that Mars has been freed. Liberated or not, Mars needs help to thrive. I stayed out of politics and supported the beings living there. But bringing this planet to its full potential would take more than freedom. Their attitude was every being for itself, and with so little to go around, it bred thievery. Everyone knew anything you could get your hands on better be tied to you if you planned to keep it.

Even our bases rooms were tiny bunker-style subterranean cells with only a single person tunnel to travel around. Being one of three females meant I was prime real estate, and everyone wanted a piece. The best I could ask for was to make friends and get into a group that would hopefully protect me.

When I noticed the two other females were lower enlisted, I made sure they were housed together. But this meant I lived alone in the officers' quarters. Eventually, my room was given a hand sensor lock which only slightly eased my tension.

On a patrol of the streets one night, I stopped to see a store owner about his business progress. I was interested in his ability to thrive in such a hostile climate. His ears were flat to his head, and he grew a flap of skin on his crown (like a rooster). A humanoid light pink skin local who sold home goods. He sweetly invited me into his shop to share some homemade wine, and I agreed. I parked my patrol buggy outside. Unbothered because of the hand sensor lock that only I could turn on.

To my surprise, I began feeling drowsy after one glass into the freshly made bottle. Forcing me to lay my head on the table when I could no longer open my eyes. Not unconscious, only unable to move.

His forehead began dripping with sweat. He giggled and clapped his hands in excitement. Then threw my body on the bed and worshipped it with his hands. He undressed me, shaking so badly he could hardly unzip my uniform. He struggled to get my boots off and tossed them behind him. With his face slightly touching me, he smelled every inch of my skin. Then rubbed me gently, titillating himself.

I knew it wasn't just the idea of sex causing his reaction; it was the entire scenario. He felt like he'd won a prize that he deserved after years of emptiness. There's no doubt he planned this for a long time, knowing he wouldn't get away with it. After assaulting my body, he dressed me. Drug me outside and struggled to get me on his lap toward the front of my vehicle. Using my hand to start the engine, he took me back to base. Where he jumped off and ran into the distance. Leaving me to sleep until someone noticed I was there.

The next day he was found, tried and sent to a manual labor camp. The kind which most beings never get out of. Proving my theory about the people there. That they're miserable to a degree we can't comprehend.

Something we don't think about often enough is the fact that on Earth we have beauty and magic in nature, even if it's the only place. It gives us hope when nothing else can. That doesn't exist there, and it leaves people hopeless and uninspired.

On our time off, we were given devices that showed our family and friends living their lives in real-time. We could watch the drama but not interact, and although I was never close with mine, I did miss the banter between relatives. The silly fighting over insignificant things that all families did. I couldn't have predicted how dicey we'd end up. How they'd never be who I could turn to about all of this, or how they may never believe it happened at all.

The sheer number of men I worked with meant a few would be bad apples. And in such a bleak environment you can imagine how sexually deprived they'd feel. Which placed a giant red target on my back. Every day walking down the hallways was nerve-racking. To see the desires of hundreds of men staring at me and not knowing if I'd safely make it across the room.

Most of the lower enlisted soldiers' jobs were creating new roads and pathways. There was high-tech equipment to cut and sort the materials but placing them on conveyor belts took hard labor. When we didn't have a use for the rock, it was sold to neighboring businesses. Since there was always tension between the warring races that would bid on the substances, their attitude about getting it to where it had to go was antagonistic. Nobody liked being a part of the excavation process.

And when they got back to base, hopped up on testosterone, there'd be a handful of sexually frustrated, who'd pay to get ahold of a memory swipe. Using it to abuse one of the few women on base. Sometimes after an attack, the men who felt guilty would implant ideas into my mind that they were there to have me memory wipe them. Lying and saying that they had a hard day, to enjoy the sex without the guilt.

Manipulated Memories

I've come to understand that what people do to each other when they are unhappy is disturbing. And in their defense, it was like holding candy in front of a baby.

The sorrow and trauma caused me to stop wearing makeup or taking care of myself altogether. Depression sunk in, and I barely survived. My fight or flight reflexes were constantly surging, and my mind would struggle later due to the strain on my systems. The intensity of my life never let up, and my body begged for a break it wouldn't get in the military.

My last couple of days on Mars were spent celebrating my promotion to Major. But the jealousy from my colleagues was painfully obvious. I didn't have the energy to argue and thankfully they hid their disdain with cheers and fake smiles. A small ceremony was held where the General of the base said some nice words. But as I stood looking out at my peers, I could feel the seething in their eyes. It was the first time I felt threatened by a promotion, since my age didn't match my insignia. But they didn't know about the secret missions and duty stations.

All I wanted was to fit in, but no matter the circumstances, I lived contradictory to what I wanted. Due to that early programming from the projects.

After my duty to Mars was over and in between duty stations I was tasked with assisting the scientists I'd worked with on Venus. A group on their home planet needed help, and they personally requested me to join their short journey.

Manipulated Memories

We took a group of sixty personnel in a battleship to a classified location many light years away.

When we showed up, it was a catastrophe I wasn't expecting. Gunfire was destroying the planet that looked like something out of the Avatar movie. City sized floating mountains and rocks covered in hanging blue and green plants, each hiding snipers. Being able to see where the firing was coming from was nearly impossible with the way the spots of land were jagged in elevation. Some soldiers had boots able to jump a football field to maneuver in between the masses. But with so much chaos it wasn't safe, they could be picked off in the air.

Unbeknownst to me, my commander had secret intel and new orders to take advantage of the situation by stealing one of the groups now poorly guarded rare mercury. Guilt ran through my bones as I realized we weren't there for the reasons I'd been told. My team suited up and landed in the middle of the massacre doing our best to render aid to anyone we could. But we were called back to the ship within minutes after a solo mission had procured the substance. I couldn't sleep for weeks from nightmares of the faces of those poor people.

It just so happens that the multiverse uses a financial system with a somewhat less destructive way to barter, since long before our planet ever existed. A point system without inflation, and multiple options of currency to be traded. And although there still was a divide in economic status, it was more so due to the species evolution. The older races could mine and use materials which would be useless to others. And of course, there was a black market where beings traded illegal activities, products and services (such as rare types of mercury).

My world became lonely and lifeless without celebrations or traditions on a ship. Punching in or out on the control panel, patrolling the area, keeping track of possible dangers, or improving morale. Every day was the same for years at a time, and the mandatory meetings were so boring it had me staring at the lines on the walls and counting their shapes. So uninterested in what anyone was saying, I'd have to be snapped back by someone saying my name.

Even the furnishings drove me nuts after a while, everything was flat and round. We couldn't have things hanging on the walls or on the tables, in case we had to hyper jump or lock down the facilities. It felt like a hospital after a while.

After the mercury debacle, I was supposed to be transported to Saturn, but I didn't want to go. And since from time to time, someone in the know about the projects would say their special phrase and get Mia back. It was worth it for them to offer me my own ship to pacify any hesitation.

Having a ship grown from my DNA was an exciting proposition I had to see. Probably the only way I would have stayed in, at the time. But my desire to move up the ranks was only to give women a spot in the councils. Working with the higher evolved beings making the big decisions for the solar system. Since the beginning of the Force, there'd only ever been a few females involved. Since I was there, I thought it'd be nice to try and move the pendulum.

To my amazement my ship grew like a child. First in a water-filled tube for around three months. Then attached to a device that tracked its progress inside a warehouse. The entire structure of the ship would expand tens of feet a day. I would sit and talk to it for hours, intuitively feeling its responses to my inquiries.

After my last promotion, I began the military dog and pony show, doing whatever it took to make the Space Force look good. Much wasn't asked of me anymore and the boredom was soul sucking.

Still, I was impressed when entering Saturn from the top, it was both breathtaking and frightening. Although a lot of the area inside the gas giant was filled with bases, I was sent to the core. Where three continent-sized compounds lived thousands of miles apart, hovering within the space. Making a triangle shape around the planet's small center. All connected by hyper-speed tunnels that allowed beings to travel long distances in minutes. Each protected by energetic domes that kept out the harsh weather.

The Gold base was currently vacant because the reptilians had locked it down. We could only marvel at the tall gaudy rectangular shiny gold architecture. The Silver base was used for team-building exercises. Housing practice obstacles where soldiers could learn to become leaders. When flying into the area from above, I could see the massive football-field size chess board with otherworldly beings figurines. I was told two teams of around thirty people would be instructed about the ten-foot-tall pieces, and on the outside were directions for starting their mini engines to move them. Forcing people to have to work together to win, which produced companionship between even the toughest egos in the universe. The bronze base was used for galactic meetings. Where beings from all over the universe came to keep tabs on the solar system. It looked and felt like it was meant for royalty. With diamond and gold buildings that shined in alternating hues of rainbow, and walkways powered by crystals lit up as direction markers. That led to holographic labels that floated atop the glittering railings of each section.

No matter who you think you are, walking through a building you can barely see the ceiling of, puts things into perspective.

Large floating sculptures of extinct species surrounded the complex, serving as reminders to the leaders of what they were fighting for.

The few times I went there, I sat in an enclosed stadium with thousands of beings to hear news about the condition of the system. Representatives would go through their findings and focus on who was looking for supplies and who'd be responsible for getting those people what they needed. As I wasn't in charge of anything yet, I was just there to watch and get used to being around higher officials. I saw that we are part of an extensive system affecting other worlds' homelands. And although the reptilians cause us problems, they're definitely not the only ones overseeing what happens here.

I was grateful to learn about the Universal workings but still devastated that I couldn't find anyone to connect with. My rank repelled people from my unit, and most other beings looked at me like a virus. Each day my depression grew, and I was on a countdown timer to emotionally explode.

Six months after they first took my DNA, my ship was ready. It was time to put her together by adding the amenities. Her main body was egg-shaped, and on each side of her were cargo holders that looked like mini versions of the craft. Round at the back and pointed towards the front. She was a small, twenty-person, well-equipped fighter ship with no intention of seeing war, at least in my eyes. We added a layer of royal blue glass-like substance on the top of the ship's shell in panes of squiggly squares for speed and cooling. The rest of the ship showed stealth grey and black.

A crew was put together for me, but I couldn't have picked better people. Each of them had something to offer the group, and I was lucky to have such a good team. Our first mission was to help out Mars with supplies. We brought food, ways to grow plants, clothing, and water purifiers.

After visiting the supply base within Saturn multiple times, I met a human man who'd been born and raised there. He'd never even been outside his small city sized location, which fascinated me. He was tall, dark, handsome and loved by everyone on board. I would visit him as often as I could, and we became close. So close in fact that it bothered my employers. I snuck him on my ship a few times, but he couldn't stand being cooped up in my room. He'd had two children from a previous marriage and a crew to run, so our love story didn't last long. Eventually his entire container was shut down and I wasn't sure if it was because of me or not, more than likely it was.

My first enlistment ended without fireworks, and I was given the opportunity for a second. But since this book is only meant to create the bones of the story itself, we're skipping ahead to the end of my life in space.

All exiting personnel were stopped at the moon to be genetically age-regressed on our way back to Earth. They placed me in a six-foot-tall cocoon-looking contraption filled with a clear goo substance with thousands of suspended bubbles. I'd spend seven hours a day inside for a week. Each night in the mirror I watched my skin grow tighter and softer, my vanity thriving as the age dial turned backwards. While automatically healing all wounds as a side effect. My intuition told me something bigger was going on, and I knew from experience not to trust the military.

The final step was to have my long-term memories blocked by what looked like an MRI machine. A monitor inside flashed pictures of my ship, mission badges, people I'd interacted with, and ET friends. As I watched the screen, tears rolled down my face.

Now that I was leaving their control, I was a threat to the Projects, the Military, and the malevolent species working with them. When I look back, it doesn't surprise me what came next. I might've done something similar if I were in their position. It's best to tie up loose ends if you can.

Let me ask you something before explaining how I got back…Where exactly do you think the inspiration for movies such as Star Trek and Star Wars comes from? Do you really think it's a made-up story that originates from nothing? What if its galactic information being shared via a human receiver? Are all the stories we believe to be myths and legends make-believe? Or are ancient civilization's writings and the imaginations of people everywhere trying to hint at what lies beyond the current grasp of reality? Could what we label as entertainment be a soft and gentle way to prepare us for expanding our understanding of possibility? Food for thought.

On the day of my reentry into my old life, an unknown technology was used to pause the timeline, using a backdoor code into the Matrix system. The entire world fell silent. The bizarre experience felt like I kept waking up from a dream. One moment, I was in a medical room being prepped for something, and the next, visual darkness. I heard soft buzzing and people scampering purposefully around me, but I was too weak to open my eyes. Someone rolled me into a vast and sterile nearby room that smelled like antiseptic. The wheels scratched against the floor, reverberating off the space around me.

My nineteen-year-old body was abducted from the barracks at Fort Lewis in the middle of the night, and brought to lay beside me, unconscious. I could feel that someone familiar was in the room, but I dared not speculate. Both of us were gently moved onto another table about six feet apart. The buzzing noise increased as we were situated under a machine. Something was placed over my head, and although I never usually was, at that moment, claustrophobia set in.

Basically, that contraption merged my consciousness with hers. Which is a nice way to say that her life force energy was ripped out and shoved into me. From my perspective, it seemed like we kept my body, but honestly, I don't know. Maybe that's how my mind handled it. What they did with the other one is anyone's guess, and a question I'd love to know the answer to.

Me trying to convince you all this happened isn't my agenda, nor is it what's important. Let's focus on what the government has already admitted to with the mind control stuff. That we just allowed them to say they stopped, like they would tell us if they did. What would be the point of top secret and classified shit if you tell people what you're doing? I'm more upset about being used as a child weapon than deciding to go with them to space as an adult.

Another thing to remember is that the space you see when you look up isn't the same space we went to. We hyper jumped through a dimensional doorway, into another universe, completely like, but not exactly our own. For some that won't seem possible or probable or scientifically plausible, but it happened.

Manipulated Memories

Elon Musk can't prove anything by going to Mars, but he can cause problems by ruining people's faith. By saying that because he doesn't see any E.T's that means there aren't any. When and if he creates the technology to jump dimensions then he can have an opinion. Until then, watch who it is you get your information from. People who work that close to A.I are not to be trusted.

Chapter 10

It's funny how historic days seem rather ordinary while you are living them.
—Dumbledore

I woke up back in my barracks as a young adult. The only hint something was wrong was a constant impending doom feeling I couldn't shake, and a higher level of anxiety. I started to see doctors and got put on pills for the troubled thoughts, but nothing made sense. I had a decent job, good boyfriend and extracurricular activities to do. Yet I was miserable.

Right before I left for space, a group of girls decided to put together a cheerleading squad for the Fort Lewis sports teams. And looking back, this could've been done to give me something to do when I got back, to keep me distracted. The base's leader even hired a professional coach, which blew my mind. Finally, a chance to have my childhood dream come true. Something the government was undoubtably aware of.

We had black, white and gold uniforms that enhanced my extreme insecurities. But I smiled and we practiced and went

Manipulated Memories

to functions all dressed up to support our team. Us girls got along great, and it was more fun than I could've imagined. We cheered for football and basketball games against the Marines and Air force before I was forced to quit.

In this timeline, I'd already been talking to my doctor about the bunions on my feet which made it painful to wear our leather boots. And since they looked horrendous as well, I was willing to do whatever it took to change them. My doctors played it off like it was no big deal to fix. Claiming I would recover and be ready to deploy in no time. Being so young meant doctors knew best, so I didn't even get a second opinion. Honestly the vanity inside me wouldn't have cared.

Alex and I had broken up right before my surgery was scheduled. I was sad and yet too tough to act like it. So, I invited one of our friends over to my apartment off base to comfort me when I was done. I knew he was married but he told me they were on a break. Something I'm sure others can relate to. I was young and heartbroken. I didn't want to think about my ex and this was how I chose to deal with it. Not my brightest moment.

They rolled me into the pre-op room and set a stack of papers on my chest. Laying on the gurney in my blue hospital gown as they said something that gives me chills now. "Sign this, to say that our students can learn on you, and you can't sue us if something goes wrong." When your government property the level of care goes right out the window. To be fair, I understand why they do this.

Manipulated Memories

I woke up with my broken foot with the bones shaved wrapped in nothing but an ace bandage. I wasn't half awake when they wheeled me out and put me in my friend's car. The meds could barely stop the throbbing pain as I attempted and failed to climb the steps to my house on crutches. Eventually needing to be carried the rest of the way. I laid on the couch and crawled back and forth to the bathroom on my hands and knees. Over and over, I took two oxycodone pills with a sip of Coors Light. Drinking more and more alcohol throughout the evening.

Let's call the fellow soldier I invited over Bryan. He showed up after work in a good mood. My roommate, him and I watched movies and drank until late into the morning. The day before I planned to have him over, I made a pact with myself. I would flirt and enjoy his company but there would absolutely be no sex happening. I was depressed from my breakup but not desperate. And although I wanted some attention, I wasn't going to sleep with someone else I worked with. That would stir up a can of worms I didn't want. So, I told Bryan my decision and he seemed cool with it.

All night he was trying harder than I expected him to, by being sweet and funny. We kissed a bunch, but I kept reminding him what the deal was. Throughout the night the more pharmaceuticals and beer I drank the drowsier I got and the less I thought about my choices. But I was enjoying the attention and lighthearted conversations we were all having.

I hadn't showered the night before because I had wanted some insurance so that I wouldn't make a bad decision. I know there are some girls out there that know exactly what I mean.

By the time I was ready for bed it was past 1a.m and I was four maybe five beers in. And who knows how many painkillers I'd had. I made the mistake of letting Bryan sleep with me on the couch. I wanted the company and didn't think anything more about it. He tried to convince me to have sex one last time before I pushed him off, turned away and fell asleep.

In the middle of the night, I woke up to his fingers inside me. I was so out of it I asked what he was doing but he had already stimulated me so much that my intoxicated body wanted sex. I pulled down my pants half asleep and he got his way. After crawling to the bathroom, I stared at the mirror. "How could this have happened? You let him sleep next to you, it's your own fault. Just act like it didn't happen and everything will be okay." All the precautions I tried to take to make sure this wouldn't happen were in vain. He knew what he was doing and now I looked like a hussy.

And like always I never confronted him about it. The embarrassment from not showering and my own judgement to let him lay with me kept me from saying anything to anyone.

The next morning my stitches started bleeding all over the floor. The boys had to take me back to the hospital to change my bandages. That's when I saw the horrendous job that was done on my foot. The laceration was jagged and thick. It didn't even make sense when looking at it. Like they had used a serrated knife to cut open my skin. My foot was swollen like a balloon and still they didn't give me a cast. I couldn't believe it, but my meekness didn't allow me to question them.

Going back to work was a nightmare. Giggles and snickering filled every room I went into. I had single handedly fueled the gossip train for months. Bryans wife called me to tell me how upset she was. And I was at a loss for words. What could I say? He had made up some story anyway. I didn't want to fight with her, and I let her rant. It felt like no one would understand what happened. So I cried myself to sleep and acted like it never happened.

Alex and I got back together and a few months later I had the second surgery on my right foot. I started noticing how good the painkillers made me feel. When they kicked in, it was like a warm hug I didn't know I needed. They became the only thing I had to look forward to. So, I ended up taking more and more throughout the days. It kept the memories of what happened dulled enough to work and live, just barely. No matter how fast I went through the bottles the doctors didn't hesitate to give me more.

My brain was flooded with frustration about my mother and the boys who made fun of me. Over time the embarrassment made me despise the Army. I hated the long hours, gross living arrangements, and feral group thought. The physical fitness and fake smiles drove me nuts. Which was only exasperated by the feeling of walking to our deaths on command, now that deployment was in the works.

Manipulated Memories

Once the doctors saw that I wasn't getting better fast enough they asked if I wanted to get out. I was ready to leave anyway and no longer wanted anything to do with the military. I was medically discharged in April 2007. At the same time, my unit left for Iraq, and the guilt I felt left me in despair. I quickly turned to self-sabotage.

I hadn't known about being blacklisted by the secret agencies, which meant I'd become part of another project to silence people like me. Marking the beginning of my encounters with their energy weapons.

Created by sophisticated computer programs that sent invisible energy waves towards the target, hidden in satellite systems or machines in vehicles. Constantly sending low vibrational frequencies towards my physical body. And since each emotion has a signature vibration, they used the waves to exaggerate my responses. They couldn't create these experiences, only bring up what was already there. Making life more unpredictable than necessary. Fear, anger, sadness, guilt could be emphasized at any moment. One day at a time, they could control my mood and thus direct my life. A long-running experiment that could prove deadly if it worked.

After leaving the military, I'd been on opiates for over two years, and since I was oblivious to their addictive nature, it left me chained to the chemical. Not once did any of the doctors ever mention physical dependency. I figured it out on my twenty-third birthday after not getting hold of my doctor and being forced to go without for over a week. Which caused horrible symptoms like nausea and fatigue to the point of lethargy. Insomnia left me delirious, and my legs would shake and cramp until it felt like the muscles were pulling off the bone. I thought I had an ulcer and checked myself into the hospital after vomiting for twelve hours straight. It took six days before they discovered that I was withdrawing from the medication. Another major timestamp in my life.

As a teenager, I had only used cocaine, speed, and ecstasy; I'd never heard of an opiate until the day of my surgery. I knew they made me feel good, and I was taking more than I needed, but I underestimated the depth of their power until that moment. A realization that single-handedly destroyed what was left of my pride and confidence. Laying in that hospital bed staring at the birthday balloons, I knew things would never be the same.

When my unit deployed, I tried having a long-distance relationship with Alex but that failed miserably. I couldn't trust myself to stay faithful, and he knew it. I was already spending too much time with a family friend and being more flirty than necessary. I was desperate for attention and knew what I was doing was wrong, and it taught me that long distance wasn't my thing.

The breakup hit me like a tsunami. And without my memories of space, it felt like we'd been together for over two and a half primarily happy years. I thought he was my best friend, strong, intelligent, and sweet, my so called first taste of a good relationship.

I was a disaster; I couldn't eat or sleep. I'd convinced myself that I'd ruined my chance with someone too good for me. The feelings ate me up inside, and I went on a chemically induced bender. My sadness only worsened as I fell into drugs and parties. Enabled by the state paying me full unemployment benefits, I continued nonstop for a year straight.

That summer became a whirlwind of doing whatever I wanted at any time. A dangerous place for a twenty-two-year-old barely adult.

During the chaos, I noticed something wrong with my mental state. Every day I felt increasingly numb to the outside world, like a hollow shell searching for something. I could fly off the handle about insignificant things and wasn't able to regulate my feelings. My personality (ego) grew, but my connection to existence faded.

I found myself needing stimulation to stay calm. Not able to go one day without chemicals of some kind, or the anxiety would eat me alive. Around the same time, I found a doctor who raised my prescription dosage, and I was incoherent most of the time. I fell asleep everywhere, at dinner with my family or talking with friends. My eyes would close mid-sentence, and my head would drop and wake me up. Super embarrassing, but I couldn't care. I'd lost the reasoning part of my mind that would prevent me from making a fool of myself. Eventually, everyone I knew stopped inviting me places.

The meds erased all need for companionship, and I became bossy and careless with outbursts and tantrums.

Manipulated Memories

Being in a comfy relationship for the last couple years meant I put on a few extra pounds. And getting back into the dating scene, had me obsessing over my insecurities.

My mind continued contrasting thoughts and mood swings. One day I would find a solution to a problem, the next, start over, confused about my own opinions. Sometimes, I'd tell Summer about feeling like a completely different person. The inability to pin down who I was, was unsettling. And my mind was hiding so many dark secrets that it was hard to process life.

For a while, I stayed with Jerry and his new wife, because I didn't want to be alone in my misery. And they watched as I began down a slippery slope with weed and pills. After leaving their house because they forced me to admit I was addicted to drugs. I attended the Art Institute of Portland nearby and moved into a bachelor pad with an older gentleman. He didn't notice that I was spiraling down, and nothing could stop it. The exterior of his house was fancy and in one of the best areas in town. Which made me think I was doing great. But inside was a party house mess, full of beer cans and weed debris.

On a random day, after lunch I had a simple but significant thought, "I could just throw up that meal and it'd be like I never ate at all." I felt compelled by the idea, and tried it, by sticking my finger down my throat and vomiting on purpose for the first time. A surge of power put a smile on my face and created a secret that was only mine. The high from the control was empowering and sneaky. I enjoyed the rush of eating as many carbs as humanly possible and then dispelling it. Getting off on the triumph of controlling my size by force. As my eating disorder progressed, I'd map out the building of wherever I went to eat with my eyes before I got my plate, making sure I could do my duty after, but people began to notice. One time, Jera took me to lunch with her boyfriend to a salad spot. I couldn't help but gorge myself because the food was delicious and when I went to throw up in the bathroom, my body wouldn't let me. I pushed my finger farther and farther down my throat, pushing as hard as I could, accidentally bursting the blood vessels in both eyes. When I looked in the mirror red splotches were swimming in both eyes, and I couldn't hide it any longer. I cleaned myself up and walked back to the table, where she told me to explain myself. I let her know what happened and her face scrunched. "That's disgusting, you're so gross. I'm not taking you out ever again. You're a fucking idiot Morgan, you look fine!"

I didn't know certain medications made it harder for me to purge, obviously I figured it out, but not in time, everyone knew. It was one more disappointment I'd never live down. Didn't matter, I couldn't please my family if I won an Oscar. They'd say it was rigged, and I didn't deserve it. I got used to the criticism, and didn't even try anymore. When it came to my family, I learned to be helpless. That's what they wanted to see, so that's what I did.

Manipulated Memories

One day I found myself standing in the bathroom, staring at my reflection in the mirror, when something shifted in my brain. As a networking specialist, I related it to a new computer program installation, like my mental functioning switched to a new operating system. Something limiting my thoughts fell away, and my philosophical perspectives of being a soldier transformed. My entire view of the Army changed. I could feel that military life was not natural. Thoughts swirled through my mind with relief of no longer being brainwashed.

At the same time, I became reckless, losing all ambition to be productive. Then like a dark comedy I was introduced to my next love. When Summers boyfriend's brother (a noted pattern) Jaylen came by the house delivering something. I was head over heels when I saw him. An instant connection formed, and there was no turning back. He was rowdy and fun with a lip piercing, short like me but tall enough to be sexy.

Both Summer and his brother tried everything they could to stop us. Which makes me laugh now because nothing would have stopped the path we were on. From day one, we spent every day together. Within weeks I dropped out of visual effects and motion graphics college, and he got fired for missing work. A tragic mess disguised as love. We enabled each other to do whatever we wanted. Having each other's back no matter how disgraceful our choices were. At least in the beginning.

Manipulated Memories

I had been trying to get off the pain meds at this point, but when I met him, he had the same addiction. To compound the story, his mother died a month after we met, leaving him a large inheritance. He was rightfully devastated, and we sank into heavy drug use. Things went from a party on weekends to hundreds of dollars a day. First on oxy's and meth, and then on heroin. A choice I deeply regretted when his entire family hated me for good reason.

Because of our constant arguing over his criminality and my mental problems, no one wanted us around. And we wore out the welcome of both our families in record time. To be together, I rented a house with a roommate from a family friend in the summer of 2010. Within a few months, Jera stopped by to visit and says she caught me hiding behind the front door with a butter knife. Which I didn't remember happening, but she was the one person I never questioned. Because the few times I tried to fight back, she kicked my ass.

Her and I had done drugs together since we were kids and yet she called the police, which blew my mind. Being up for a few days and fighting with Jaylen left me highly intoxicated. So, there wasn't anything I could say to defend myself, but I wasn't hurting anyone or causing trouble.

That was my first arrest, so the officers let me shower and prepare for jail. I used meth for an hour in the bathroom while Jera told the officers about the stolen car parts in the basement. Snitching out Jaylan with no mercy. I walked out of the shower to hear the conversation and predicted the problems it would cause me in the future. There was no choice but to agree when they found the evidence. I knew he would retaliate.

It was my first stint in county jail and another timestamp in my life. Disabled veteran one day without even a speeding ticket, the next a convicted felon. It felt like someone came into my home and took my chance at a normal life. A grudge I would hold onto for years. I didn't understand that my fate was already sealed by my choices. I was let out after seven days with two years of probation.

A couple weeks later at three in the morning, I huddled on the couch in the fetal position, berating myself for the drugs I'd taken. I'd been alone and up for days struggling to keep my eyes open from fear of the shadows. My poor body swimming with amphetamines barely able to function. I heard a distant rustling, and my senses went into overdrive focusing on the silence, searching for any sign of what it could be. My heart pounded loudly in my chest and the sound rang again in my ears. Exaggerated by the eerie quiet. I assured myself it was just the drugs. The fear rattled my body when the sound happened again, and I sat up. It was dark, and there was no way in hell I was going to check out what it was. As a precaution I turned off the sound of my phone. While shaking, I got up and made it three steps before I heard it again, louder this time.

Some kind of intense rummaging through something was happening in the basement, the one place I never went in the house. Freaked out, I held my breath and decided to run back to the safety of the couch and say aloud, "Take whatever you

Manipulated Memories

want." Over and over, I told myself, "It's all in your head. You're tired and need to sleep." I laid my head down on the couch arm unable to stay awake any longer. But was soon startled awake by a spiritual nudge. I opened my eyes and saw smoke billowing out from a grate on the floor in front of me. I hopped up, confused. Carbon monoxide, dioxide, and particle matter were filling the room. My house was on fire!

I stumbled into the kitchen to get a bag for my belongings more alert than I had any right to be. Then ran top speed into my room clumsily throwing things around looking for clothes and necessities. When I stopped for a brief second and recognized that the heat was centered there, coming from the basement. My eyes began to burn, and I was only able to find a few items in the panic. I gave up and ran straight out the front door to throw the trash bag outside. Luckily my car was parked close to the house that day.

I sprinted around the back of the house to get my roommates two German shepherds. Recognizing that they were supposed to warn us of intruders but didn't. I stuffed their big bodies into the back of my tiny two-door Honda as fast as I could. And as I closed the door, I had a thought. "Did I just leave all my drugs on the coffee table?" Oh shit!

I dashed back inside as the entire house filled with smoke. Ducking my head and covering my face, while grabbing the glass pipe and paraphernalia, so the cops didn't find it later.

Within minutes the police and fire department showed up in a blaze of glory, and the officers took my statement. After the shock wore off, I appreciated the genuine caring demeanor of the people working on the scene. After waiting for hours, my roommate came home to take the dogs. I told them how curious it was that the fire was directly underneath my room. Exactly where Jaylen had left the stolen car parts. Was that a coincidence?

"Do you have anywhere you can go?" the firefighter asked. With my head down, I teared up and said, "No." They immediately called the Red Cross services and had me a hotel room down the street for three days within hours. It was early morning now, and my nerves were shot. I needed rest.

After checking in, I fell asleep the moment I laid my head on the pillow. Sleeping better in hotels than in my own space. Crashing out for nearly twenty hours of much needed sleep. Jolted out of my meth coma by a knock at the door the next day. Still half-awake, or I'd never have opened that door. I thought of myself as a better criminal than that.

The officers checking on me were convinced I had set the fire on purpose. A completely different attitude than I was expecting. I thought they'd protect me after what happened. Instead, they saw I'd been arrested a couple weeks back, which automatically made it my fault.

The bias of police officers against drug addicts is one subject I know a lot about. It's heartbreaking how they don't care about millions of people struggling. When shady stuff happens, they blame the user without merit. Innocence until proven guilty is a lie, and people must reevaluate our use of the judicial system.

They began asking me stupid questions like, "Did you paint demons on the walls with paint?" I thought they were kidding, but it made sense later when I thought about the potential connection to the Illuminati. Not to mention the likelihood that someone could've been encouraged by the Mk-ultra leaders for another test. It's possible they weaponized Jaylen's love for pyrotechnics and mischief, mixed with his own desire to protect himself.

Since I had a prior arrest, I was lawfully searched and sent back to jail with a second felony for the drugs they found hidden in a sack of rice crispy treats. Now that I was seen as a criminal and deviant, I decided to be exactly that. In my mind that meant to do as many chemicals as possible in the most potent way. Finding like-minded "friends" that were into needles was the next step in my journey.

To all my curious friends who play with narcotics, please don't ever take your drug use this far. The misery this created for me was soul-crushing. I know most people experiment, and honestly, I'm not against that. But this level of physical destruction to my body was horrific. Don't do it.

I asked my latest dealer and his cronies questions like, "Why do you like doing it that way?" Their answers intrigued me when they said it felt different and stronger, and enhanced the sex they could have for hours, which I didn't understand. "How can anything change how it feels to have sex?" They didn't know, but they'd piqued my interest, and I demanded to be shown how to do it myself.

Manipulated Memories

They reluctantly suited me up a syringe full of crystal meth. That nearly gave me an orgasm when it hit my system. Sometimes the reaction made me throw up (which meant it was good stuff), and every time I took a hit, I'd cough and laugh. I loved how I instantly felt powerful and alert. I thought it was the answer I'd been searching for, and I'd follow it anywhere. Let us call that the destruction of what was left of my moral judgment.

After the fire, I began noticing that my life was being systematically destroyed by one catastrophe after another. When these things happen, we always have choices, but I couldn't see the other options through my rage. A mountain of anger and intense childhood trauma came to the surface with a vengeance, and I decided to give up on life entirely. My ego was emotionally hollowed out, which caused my warrior to have to take over. I began to call myself by my middle name, as a way to distinguish that I was no longer who I used to be.

I moved into the walk-in closet of that dealer's house and spent my days staring at surveillance camera footage or peeking through the blinds in the living room. Terrified of nothing and waiting for the apocalypse. My unemployment ran out and being too high to work meant I had to steal hundreds of dollars' worth of stuff from stores to sell. Food, clothing, and accessories were my favorite. I'd become a typical drug addict statistic, and I knew it. When needles became my preferred method, all bets were off. I lost all boundaries in a matter of months. Proud at times of what I'd stolen. Small victories against the society I hated so much. I didn't feel guilty since the store would get reimbursed anyway. Never once connecting my actions to their effects on my life.

The thing about drugs is that they give an intense mind and body euphoria, with fake joy and happiness that numbs the emotional system, so you can't see your problems anymore. Speed sends a vortex of activation energy into all senses. All touch felt amazing, but my sexual issues from the abuse never let me enjoy it.

I obsessed and focused so intently on one thing I never got anything done. Making hundreds of lists and never checking anything off. I was planning extravagance and living in poverty. Surrounding myself with a fantasy of possibility that comforted the sadness. I forgot appointments, birthdays, and meetings. I avoided anyone who didn't use, which pushed me further into solitude and insanity.

Heroin was a body melting seductress. The physical easement and relief it gave were enticing and dangerous. A swollen ego and false confidence kept me chasing the delusion. It took over my body in less than three days, hijacking the ability to function without it. A fight between logic and physical pain was a lose-lose. The chemical waste buildup in my system caused severe damage, and I have scars all over my body from injection mishaps and abscess removals. My hands and arms are riddled with marks that'll never go away. A souvenir of the lifestyle I chose. A space in my life that was dripping with darkness.

Manipulated Memories

I stayed to myself and opted to be quiet. Jaylen tried to shield me from the madness when he was around, and when things were good, we were best friends. We laughed so much my stomach hurt, because he was a jokester with high energy even when he didn't feel good. He wore his hat brim tipped up with a skater aesthetic and road BMX with his friends. I loved that he was fun and courageous.

As we spiraled downward, we took turns as drivers and thieves. First, we'd choose a store; my favorite was Fred Meyer's and his was Home Depot. We'd plan out what to get and sometimes have requests from our dealers. If we didn't just fill an entire grocery cart and walk out the front door, either he put items into his coat, or I put them in my purse. The driver for that day would leave a few minutes early and bring the car around. For a while, it worked like a charm, doing it any other way had a higher chance of getting caught. When I was too sick to go in, he got arrested, which broke my heart.

One time during a breakup I ran back to my dads with my tail between my legs, angry that I'd let myself live that way. And after rummaging through the mess in my car I noticed the driver door panel looked strange. Out of curiosity and intuition, I pulled it off without as much effort as it should've taken. To see four syringes filled with heroin, he'd been hiding from me, in my own car. I wasn't a saint either and would give myself more than him whenever I could, but that wasn't as often as I would've liked.

Manipulated Memories

Whenever he went to jail, I'd notice more black SUVs than normal. I intuitively knew someone was watching me, but my drug-induced paranoia gave me a great excuse to ignore it. Two of them pulled up beside me one day when I stopped at a store. As I walked back to my car, something was off, and turning the key didn't start the engine. I was convinced it was Jaylen because we were in a fight, but I'd find out it was the project's minions. I had to call for help to get someone to show me that the battery was disconnected.

Somehow, I never got caught stealing, but I did go back and forth to jail a dozen or so times from 2010 to 2014, mostly for evading probation or dirty UA's. Every police officer in my county knew me by name, and it wasn't a compliment.

At first, jail was intimidating, but eventually, I made friends with the girls on the block, and sang to help others feel better. While getting to know the system, I heard about the corrupt and inhumane conduct between police and inmates, and the abuse of power throughout the entire justice department. With extreme sentencing habits for judges that held drug addicts as menaces to society.

They didn't understand the pain that created the behavior, and it saddens me that drug use is villainized. Using a substance to feel better shouldn't be an automatic sentence. I wish society would look into the psychology of why people turn to drugs in the first place. Doing crimes and using substances are not intrinsically linked. Many people use some kind of substance (prescribed by doctors, literally the same thing) and are not dangerous, But the moment you say an illegal chemical was involved, that person is no longer credible. A flawed opinion and ignorant judgment.

After most arrests while on probation, I'd be put into a treatment center or sober living, which required specific details on how to live my life, including seeing a probation officer every week. At the time, that was impossible. I was still a good person who wouldn't have harmed a soul if I hadn't had to, but I had to survive. Without friends and family to help me, I was alone in a sometimes-dangerous world. I wanted to change, and every day I tried the best I could to be the person I knew I could be, but I didn't have any money or anywhere to go when I was released most of the time. So, I'd desperately try finding Jaylen, which was nearly impossible and rarely happened after a while.

Once I became a criminal, I felt like people could smell it. Like something about me was inherently wrong. It took my self-esteem through the shredder, and my heart closed off. Then the drug reactions told my mind I was unsafe. Everyone outside my small entourage became a threat. The drugs enhanced the psychic abilities I didn't know I had. Instead, I accepted that I was crazy. Then manifested more of those symptoms from the constant thoughts that I was insane. I became another institutionalized mental patient. Needing ten psych meds a day to keep it together became just as much of an addiction as anything else. My ill-advised doctors convinced me I wasn't okay if I didn't have my crazy pills.

On one of my last stints in county, my P.O. placed me in a work-release center while living in a locked down facility at night. I lasted three weeks before Jaylen found me, and I bailed, immediately on the run looking for drugs. We stopped at a fast-food bathroom to use our procured heroin, but being more affected by it since I was sober for the last few months meant overdosing on a tiny amount.

Years later I would remember what happened as I lay unconscious. Learning that I slowly floated above the ceiling of the restaurant. I noticed the freedom from the physical body and yet was dazed and unclear about what was happening. I didn't feel any sense of urgency or worry that I was watching my body be hauled away on a gurney. Within a few moments a masculine energy guided me to a interdimensional door. I opened it with curiosity and blankness. It led me to a room with fourteen large TV monitors stacked on top of each other and one chair, that he pointed at sternly. I knew I was in trouble by the look on his face. I was forced to sit and watch a reenactment of my recent life. He said he was disappointed and told me to get it together, or life was going to get much harder. I bowed my head in shame and shrugged my shoulders while apologizing. As I stood up from the seat he pushed me hard back into my body.

I woke up in the ER with an impending doom feeling that I had almost royally messed up. Although I should've been devastated that I'd nearly lost my life, I was determined to leave the hospital and get high again. The staff made me sign a paper saying I could die if I fell asleep in the next twelve hours. So, Jaylan did some favors for his 'friends' to keep me awake with speed for the rest of the night. I only point this out to show the complete disconnect between a rational person and what I'd become. Addiction isn't about drug users wanting to party. It's a clear and significant cry for help.

We should look into creating communities that accept people while they're using. Society should stop pointing, laughing, and turning their noses up about something they know nothing about. It's important to remember that no one has any more or less value than anyone else.

I met some of the most amazing people during this time. Singers, writers, painters, and poets. Deeply feeling individuals abused as children, who didn't know how to cope with their emotions. Let these centers teach people how to accept themselves as they are, high or not. Stop villainizing millions of people who want to soothe the pain inside them.

Most people do something else if they don't turn to chemicals. Overeat, beat their family, buy too much, talk too much, or drive too fast. Which is not in any way different than people who learned that chemicals do what they say they are going to do; make them feel better. I know that if I didn't have drugs at this time, I couldn't have handled the pain of life.

Chapter 11

Some people are easier targets than others.
~M.J

After breaking up and getting back together for the hundredth time, Jaylen and I started living in my two-door Honda Civic over the next few months. Taking turns driving when the other was incarcerated. Spending all day stealing, waiting for hours on our drug dealers, or scoping out creative places to hide the car while we slept (if we slept). Only to wake up in the morning sick, rushing to the nearest McDonald's to pee, and do it all over again. We couldn't seem to leave each other even though the more time we spent together, the worse it got. In a way, it taught me to be self-sufficient. Not that what I was doing was right, but it felt like my only option. So, I did what I had to do.

By now, I was tired of the insanity, and we found an ad on craigslist for a super cheap room to rent. Having us move into a three-bedroom apartment with other drug users. I lost my car in the dead of winter when the E-brake we used as a regular break went out. Sliding us into oncoming traffic in the middle of a four-way stop on ice. Right in front of a cop. Once again Jaylen got arrested for warrants, and I went home defeated.

A couple weeks later, he came back to the house. To find that I'd been so desperate for heroin, hoping the toxic water had opiates in it, muscled (injected straight into the fatty tissue) a colony of bacteria into my right leg. It had swollen up, creating two baseball-sized abscesses (infections). I lied and said I was fine, limping around town searching for drugs for a couple days before my entire quad doubled in size. Unable to move, I begged for help from the pain. We argued and I could tell he felt bad for not being able to help me. He was so upset he left the house, and I wouldn't see him again for many years. I had to stumble my way down our stairs and ask a neighbor to call the ambulance. When I got to the hospital, the doctors told me I was hours away from losing my leg.

Now that he was gone for good, I took another turn for the worse. Since he left me without closure, I became obsessed with finding him. I couldn't help but search for him in every car for years. I felt dead inside, convinced I'd never love anyone else. My ability to take care of myself dwindled, and I stepped farther into darkness.

I'm not proud, but I'm not ashamed to tell you I paid for drugs or money with my body multiple times after that breakup. I didn't care about life anymore; he was my everything. We were so enmeshed as a couple that I didn't have a personality or an identity without him. I had nothing.

Manipulated Memories

I met a new heroin dealer who'd become my number one supplier right before Jaylen left me, and in the beginning, he gave me drugs just to hang out with him. Since after paying rent, I was broke, we spent a lot of time together. He was probably around sixty years old but looked older due to his lifestyle.

Usually, I could throw make-up on and wear something nice, and no one would notice my thieving. But now I was a walking manikin, and I felt like I had no choice. So, I ended up servicing him around five times within a few months. Mainly because he paid well, and I was desperate. I was so high I couldn't keep track of the days anyway. Out of my mind, roaming back and forth from his house to mine. Hiding from the world until I had to make a run again. These incidents were rare, while in a very hopeless place. I don't blame or look down on myself for this part of my life. It was a short-lived, rock-bottom type of place where girls who need money consider this option. I'm not unique.

Honestly, I don't know why I put half this information in this book, but I feel compelled to believe that someone will find comfort in my truth. And I want to own everything I've been through in case someone tries to use it against me. I was tired, hungry, sick, broke, and eventually, I couldn't keep it together. When my lease was up, I moved in with that drug dealer and was high 24-7. For hours I would sit in the bathroom with a syringe full of meth or heroin. Over and over, using the same needle, unable to hit a vein due to dehydration. My arms would drip with blood after numerous attempts, and if I couldn't get it in, I felt like the entire world would end.

Getting high was the only way I could tolerate life anymore. Each shot promised the intense misery would disappear if only for a brief moment. Once I saw blood flash in the needle time stopped, and relief rushed over me before it even hit my system. A never-ending world of pain and intoxication. The stress of the needle use was more than it was worth, but it had a death grip on me. My mind was convinced it was the only way we would find the magical sensation of our first time. But by the end, it began to be more exhausting to be high all day than sober. Everything was backwards, and I was pitiful.

My best attempt at finding a solution was to relocate, so I moved to San Diego where Jera was. Although I knew we were like oil and water, I held onto the hope that I could mend the sibling bond. My head rested on the window seal as the smelly, packed Greyhound bus drove down the I5 freeway. Each stop had me wondering if I'd like it there. The movies made it seem magical, and my natural optimism wanted to believe that. Anything was better than what I was doing back home.

I knew Jera would be looking her best and I dreaded seeing her. My clothes barely fit I was so thin.

When we pulled into the station and I unloaded my stuff, I fell in love with southern California at first sight. Jera raved about the Drum and Bass clubs and festivals (the one type of music we both loved) with her usual side of pessimism. As we drove to her house, she pointed out things to do in the area. The beaches, the people, the nightlife, and I saw the separate planet that is California. The palm trees and warmth made it sexy. The six lane highways said it could be both violent, and welcoming. And for me the saltwater smell in the air was inspiring.

The first thing on my agenda was to get sober, so I signed up for a thirty-day rehab at the La Jolla VA Medical Center. While sitting in a circle with a handful of other vets, I learned about addiction. I said what every counselor and therapist wanted to hear, with good intentions. But they didn't know I was a professional chameleon. I did want all the things they said I could have, like a normal life. But that was years away and by then normal wouldn't be an option. Since Jera and I couldn't get along for more than a few days I decided to move into a sober living house up north when I finished.

But sometimes old habits die hard, and within a month, I called another veteran who'd relapsed from the hospital and had him pick me up. He rented a hotel room where we got high on meth continuously for seven days. Most men in those types of situations hoped I'd become a sexual wild person once I got high, but they'd be horribly disappointed. And that time was no different. I knew he wanted it but that'd always been a touchy subject for me. I knowingly pressed my luck by being around people expecting something I wasn't willing to give, but my naivety thought it wouldn't be a problem. I only slept with people I liked or needed something from, and that was few and far between.

Manipulated Memories

I did know that that was the only reason he gave me free drugs. But, instead, I rummaged through my belongings or drew pictures for hours, barely able to speak. The stimulation quieted my anxiety, and usually I took advantage by staying to myself and scrolling.

By the eighth day, I was so exhausted that I had to lay on the bed. I tried to rest but couldn't. My senses were on fire, and I could feel something wasn't right. When he began acting strangely, talking to himself out loud, inching towards and away from me on the bed. While repeating sentences that didn't make sense. I was obviously concerned and scared of what might happen. But I was too high to leave or find help. He stood up from the bed and confessed that he soon wouldn't be able to stop his desire to have sex. I was alarmed but too intoxicated to leave with nowhere to go.

My ego was too proud to ask Jera for help knowing she would make my life hell if I did. So, I sat frozen in fear, masking it with apathy. Acting like everything would be fine, without any proof it would be. To ease my discomfort, he invited over a female friend. Her dark curly hair was as beautiful as she was. We talked for an hour before heading to the hot tub downstairs. It was late into the night by then and her presence did help me relax a little bit. The warm water and chemicals attracted me to her, and I began to let loose. We made our way out of the water and back into the room, relieved and in a better mood.

Right when I was starting to feel at ease with my predicament, she started to pour fake blood, (at least I hoped it was) over her neck and body. The strangest thing I'd ever seen. Maybe that kind of thing would be less wild at a metal concert, but no one was even talking to each other at that point. She just stood in a mirror looking at herself, dripping red all over her bikini. I watched it in amazement.

She asked me to hand her my phone, and I reluctantly did. After I got it back, I saw she'd put cryptic words and creepy pictures on my contacts. When she spoke, it was in riddles, and her aura seemed sinister, her motives unclear. Something told me to leave, but when she asked me if I wanted to get away from the guy there, I said yes. For some reason willing to go wherever she was going.

After becoming clairvoyant, I saw what was happening to people when they took drugs. Crystal meth happens to open the body's protective energy field. It allows in demons who take over certain brain functions. These demons stay attached to the user and continuously torture and torment them with thoughts and ideas. Enticing the possessed to do and say things they normally wouldn't. Doctor's want to say that the drug disrupts the brain's pleasure and reward centers which makes them act poorly. Which may be true, but life has many layers, and the physical body is only one. It's a spiritually ignorant conclusion that only considers the third dimension. Drug addicts are indeed talking to and interacting with demons all day long.

Within minutes someone nicknamed Tiny was knocking on the door, like he'd been lurking nearby. If I'd thought about how weird that was, I wouldn't have made the worst judgment call of my life. Leaving to a place I'd never been with two people I didn't know. On the ride, Tiny claimed he was Italian, but he looked Spanish. Around forty-five, short, and overweight. After dropping the girl off, I was alone with him for the first time. I passed out after doing some of his drugs and woke up on a floor at an unknown location, with a person lying next to me, unable to move, watching a TV. Within seconds the world went black and sometime later, I woke up on a bed with Tiny watching me. Within minutes, he claimed to have recently killed ten people after his wife's murder. Saying it like it was nothing. Joking and giggling about how strange it was. Telling me he slept in a shed to hide from the cops. All I could do was stare at him, in shock. I changed the subject to dispel my fear and we chatted about random things. But in the background my mind was trying to figure out how I'd get out of there.

I didn't know or care if what he said was true, it didn't matter. I was on full alert and stranded. Something in my mind snapped to attention, activating fawn mode to protect me, and I knew I wasn't going anywhere. After he assured me that I 'could stay with him as long as I needed' I knew without him saying the words, he meant, you are mine. I was in a mind-controlled mess, and I knew it. It was brilliant yet evil, and it spun me for a loop. I lived in terror for six months, willing to do whatever I had to to survive. The fawn response tried to convince me I wanted to be there, and at times it did, but I knew deep down what was going on and sometimes I got spurts of courage. I was a twenty something naive girl who thought she could work people to get what she wanted, now in way over her head. I had to act normally and talk to my friends and family like nothing was wrong. But inside, I was convinced I'd be losing my life. My mind made up stories about what he'd do. The fear he'd find me and hurt me like the others kept me from trying to leave on my own.

When he didn't have a shirt on, I could see the tattoos of two revolvers on each side of his back torso and the skeleton overlay down his spine. The drugs and stress had me sleeping for days. After that, I realized four other people lived in the house. I couldn't tell you what their arrangement was, but I was ignored. It was a classic drug house, dirty and neglected, that smelled like metal and meth. I was contained in a small room in the back of the house filled with piles of car parts, and a giant bed that occupied the rest of the space. We acted like an average couple, although it was a freak show. Inside my mind, I kept hearing, "Give in to the darkness completely. You're going to die. Let the darkness in. He's going to murder you. He's going to kill you today. Don't go to sleep." Over and over, words of torment riddled my thoughts. Now I know I was being messed with through dark magic, but I wasn't aware of the possibility at the time, I thought I was going crazy. My muscles couldn't relax, and I sat on the edge of sanity.

I was never handcuffed, but the terror of being killed kept me from going anywhere. When I did leave with him, we did terrible things and put ourselves in dangerous positions. Within the first three months, I felt a shift in my brain again.

Manipulated Memories

The rage, confusion and discomfort I was in changed something in me, and I succumbed to the idea I'd end up in a body bag. Being mentally caged with no chains did a number on my psyche. Plus he was obsessed with me, thinking he was in love, and tried to please me sexually, which was unbearable. My consciousness had to leave the body just to survive the disgust. I was no longer that nice and innocent girl. I was on a journey of destruction. The mind games he played had me disillusioned about what reality was. By saying he was protecting me and that I needed him. That the world was out to get me, and I wasn't safe.

He took me to houses where children were being abused, and I had no way to help them. It was psychological torture, and my eyes were pulled wide open to the shadows hiding under this beautiful planet's surface. He kept tabs on my every move, even forcing me to shower with him. Desperate to have a moment of privacy, I locked the door to the bathroom by pulling out the drawer that prevented it from opening. Rather than leave me alone, he ripped the door in half by punching and kicking it in. Then grabbed me by the throat and held me against the mirror.

At that exact moment, his mother walked into the house, and I still see it like it was yesterday. Me pinned to the glass with his hands around my neck. She pleaded to me from the hallway, "Morgan, you're going to have to calm down."

If you want to see a world of evil, I promise you it does exist. By catching reflections of demons in the mirrors, I saw the evidence of the sorcery taking place behind the scenes.

Keeping me in constant fear and unable to leave. Things did not add up there, and he'd alter personalities and rage out for no reason, then be perfectly fine ten minutes later.

We were even pulled over twice in a stolen car, and my out of state warrant didn't get the cops to take me in. I tried carrying post it notes in my pocket that said: "Help Me!" But he was always one step ahead, never taking me around anyone who'd listen. Twice I was taken to the looney bin when I tried to leave but walked around confused with nowhere to go. I told the hospital what was happening, but they gave me more meds and released me to him. I know that most doctors mean well, but this was tragic. I was losing all cognitive functions from the intensity of the fear and didn't want to live, yet I knew I couldn't give up.

I finally got the courage to talk to one of the other men who lived in the house. Sitting next to him, crying, I asked if he was planning to help Tiny kill me. But he didn't say anything, just laughed and smoked on his meth pipe. While I was there, Tiny would allow me to have a small amount of meth throughout the months with him. But he only gave me enough to make me want more. It was enraging, yet I didn't have any income or room for an opinion. One time around Christmas, he got some bad dope (or he gave me fake stuff on purpose) and my entire body began to itch with fervor. I couldn't move as my skin turned red from head to toe. I had to stand up with my arms out while he cut up an aloe plant from the front yard and smeared it all over my sickly body.

Manipulated Memories

The whole time I was there I knew I had a settlement coming from a car accident. It was my only chance out and either the end of me or my freedom. The night before I had the worst panic attack of my life. The next day I would receive my check, and it could be my last. My mind told me it would have worked perfectly for my assailant to get rid of me after it came in. I laid in the fetal position for hours, crying. When a giant transparent hand made of gold and white light came through the window like it wasn't even there, covering my entire body in its palm. I couldn't move or react, while its fingers cradled me like a child. Relieving for a moment the pain and inspiring me to send an email to my youngest sister Cally. Telepathically telling me to tell her what happened. I never told her that she saved my life, by being a person I could trust.

Once again, I didn't think about the paranormal aspect of what happened. I couldn't process any more than what I was already dealing with. I waited for him to leave the house and got out the email and phone call. It was worth the risk, even though I wasn't sure what he'd do when he found out, I told her where I was, giving her his name and address so they could find me. There was nothing he could do after that; I had won. Not only did he have to let me go, but he had to do it without making a scene. For the first time, I saw that the universe had my back. I was put on a bus back to San Diego unharmed physically. But, when I got on the bus, I saw a middle-aged blonde man following me, who made sure I noticed. Terror plagued my dreams and smells tortured me

Manipulated Memories

when they reminded me of Tiny. And I had one more reason to think my life had become a cosmic joke.

Chapter 12

Meanness is incurable; it cannot be cured by old age, or by anything else.
~Aristotle

After hours on a bus, I made it back to Jera's and her boyfriend Phills, forever changed. My ability to function was overloaded with confusion, so I chose not to tell her what I'd been through. They assumed I was on a six-month bender. I let them believe whatever they wanted, because I lacked the energy to fight off their judgment. I was too mentally paralyzed by the trauma to talk about it anyway. Unable to converse with them or make necessary decisions. Incapable of eating or sleeping naturally for weeks. I mostly sat in the backyard staring at the trees.

In the background, wanting me closer to the area, the project leaders subliminally suggested I move back to Washington. Giving me false hopes of looking for something familiar that could soothe my soul. Always desperately searching for a magic happy pill or person to save me. I jumped from one friend's house to another, living only to escape the pain, and grasping on to anyone who'd allow me.

Manipulated Memories

When I got back to Portland, I wasn't any better, and me having some cash didn't help. I knew Summer had turned to drugs like me over the years. So we spent some time together and got high off and on, but both of us were a mess. She was dating a women beating drug dealer at the time which helped when I didn't have money. But now we were so deep into the lifestyle that neither of us were of any use to the other.

After staying with her for a few days, some drug friends invited me to meet a young man at a taco bell. I was interested in him right away, and I could tell he felt the same. But I was so nervous and high that I left a five-hundred-dollar money order on the tray when I threw away my food. Too embarrassed and paranoid to go back and get it. Another proof of my ridiculousness. He enticed me with his mysteriousness. His dark skin and tattoos were sexy, and I was smitten. He was troubled, reckless, and uncontrollable, my favorite. There was something about him that was magnetizing and enchanting. Together we did drugs and wrote music, reminiscing about our past and connecting on a deeper level.

The last night I saw him, after getting high and having sex, I fell asleep. Waking up to what seemed like a different person. He was now by himself on the couch, which hurt my heart. And it was strange that he had a backpack sitting next to him. Something about the tone in his voice was off, and he began saying hateful things. I overheard him invite people on a phone call, insinuating he was bored of me. The energy in the house shifted drastically when one of his friends tried to hint that I should leave. Pointing out that he was not who I thought he was. I endured the belittlement and stepped outside to smoke a cigarette, trying to understand what was happening. Walking back into the bedroom, I saw that the dish I kept my drugs in was miraculously full. Knowing good and well, I'd finished my stash hours earlier.

Obviously, when it came to my drug addiction, it controlled me and not the other way around. Overlooking the minor mix-up was a wish come true. These guys were weird, and I wanted to numb out. I did it all in one shot with a harpoon size needle. My brain started feeling heavy and disconnected, and paranoia engulfed me. The boys turned the music up and started jumping around like kids. Then ripped down a hanging American flag taped to a wall, exposing a three-foot-tall pyramid with an eye in the center while deviously laughing, and I was officially creeped out.

One of the men I didn't know told me to leave in a harsh manner. With nowhere to go I mentally froze while sitting outside his house for hours, contemplating what to do. Fear curdled in my stomach when they wouldn't open the door or speak to me. Then, something shifted, and I was overcome by a feeling of imminent danger. I searched the area for any kind of weapon. Rummaging through old toolboxes and barrels for anything sharp, heavy, or blunt. I scrounged up two old switchblades and put one in each hand, with the exposed blades running through my middle fingers, holding the casing in my fist. The bleeding would be the price of concealment if necessary and pain wouldn't have registered anyway. It was pitch black outside, and I was stuck in a remote farm-type location. Far enough from people that you had to search to find them.

This incident marked the forced opening of my psychic abilities to the next level. And I was defenseless because of ignorance and vulnerable to the dark energies surrounding us all. My mind went into autopilot, back to my military training out of necessity. I could hear beings teasing and berating me with vile exploits and comments from a different dimension. They reminded me of past faults and failures, picking me apart from the inside with whispers, begging me to kill myself. Explaining how horrible of a person I was and why I didn't deserve to live. Suggesting that people were out to get me. Then laughing at how weak I was for not being able to do it. Using the voices of loved ones to convince me of their authenticity, urging me to give up. Talking about my abortions, calling me evil and pathetic. Throwing words of damnation all over my already deteriorating world. I was alone in the woods on a very bad trip. Whatever they'd given me wasn't going to get better before it got worse.

With proper discernment everyone can easily combat this bleeding through of energies and protect themselves. But I wasn't aware of how to do that yet so I was now interacting with beings that wished violence upon me, and there was nothing I could do about it.

Evil spirits pounded on the walls of my mind screaming my name. Barking orders for me to knock on the doors of random people's houses. Oscillating between instructing me like a friend trying to help and incessantly insisting like a drill sergeant. Telling me they knew I was coming. My eyes darted back and forth through the blackness of night, searching for anything that could save me, switching between paralyzed and provoked. I couldn't reach my own thoughts through the sea of noise. And I wanted to just lay down and die, but that wasn't my style.

The military taught me to be a good soldier, and what do good soldiers do? They do what they are told. So, I inched my way to the nearest porch light and stood for minutes staring at it. A part of me believed the lies I was hearing, and the bigger part knew better. Those aspects fought each other in words as I decided to see if they were right. I brushed my hair out of my face and tried to not look high on whatever that was. I tucked the knives into my purse while being impressed that I still had it around my shoulder.

Then one by one I knocked on doors in the cold. Can you imagine the faces of the people I woke up at three a.m? So confused that the only words I could get out were, "Can I use your phone?" I had a phone, and I didn't have anyone to call, but I couldn't think of anything else to say in the heat of the moment. Once my ego was the size of a pea I recoiled into the woods. Crawling through the mud for another twelve hours, looking for a hiding place, continuing the battle of not giving in to the madness. My character was taken to the dark side, and I was left to roam the country alone. Running from unseen forces that followed me everywhere.

Manipulated Memories

To top off the situation I had a SUV full of so called officials, laughing and teasing, while collecting the data of my response to the drugs. It's sad what a perfect lab rat I was, since I had no backbone. I never questioned the possibility that I was being manipulated. Because doctors had been telling me I was crazy for years. And I trusted the medical community like so many others. Even though they had absolutely no idea what they were talking about. To anyone who sees and hears things not of this world, please trust me that you are not crazy. Doctors are the ignorant ones, and you can protect yourself.

One of the guys from the night before came looking for me the next morning. When he found me sitting on the ground shivering, he took me to his house, put something in my drink, and molested me while sleeping. He proceeded to act like my friend for three days. Allowing me to crash at his home in a small makeshift room in the attic.

On the fourth day he gave me a letter admitting he had sexually assaulted me when I was asleep. Then to top it all off, he confessed that he was paid to kill me but couldn't. I tried to get him to answer my questions about it, but he wouldn't respond to them. My mind went straight to thinking it was Tiny who had the hit out this time. But all he said was I couldn't stay in Portland any longer, and without any choice in the matter, I was off again.

After that night, I thought little about it. My best way to deal with emotions was to ignore them. Later in the story, I will learn to heal through meditation and energy work. Until then, I kept everything to myself and quickly descended into depression. I shamed myself for these awful attacks, like I asked for it.

This life I'd been living wasn't living at all. It still felt like I was going from one traumatizing event to the next. A walking statistic who couldn't take care of herself. Sad and lonely no matter who was around. Randomly staring off in the distance, replaying these memories, and almost telling everyone.

Hiding from the pain took a toll on me. I found myself either sick from doing too many or not enough drugs. The constant struggle to find a suitable substance to cover up the emotions was exhausting. A full-time job that played out twenty-four hours a day all year. Cocaine for the sadness, heroin for the self-loathing, meth for the melancholy, and weed if I didn't have anything else. The only job that takes everything you have with no return. A separate functioning world just under the surface of society's white picket fence. This career required careful networking and event planning. Marketing teams for promoting and testing products. We even had our own laws and requirements for service on the streets. The system was flawed but honored more often than not.

I'd have a box full of five different substances set up in neat little containers when times were good. Each one lined up by importance or potency. Only content when I had more than enough for the week, and the rare times that happened I was consumed with arrogance and pride. Feeling like I'd won the lottery, and nothing could bother me. I made calls I shouldn't have and spent time with people I didn't want to, just to have something to do. I blasted my stock stereo to Drake music and sang at the top of my lungs, thinking nothing could kill my vibe. I lived in a hazy fantasyland that no one else could see. It didn't matter if I nodded out on the freeway or jumped lanes of traffic at the last minute, I was invincible. Giggly, proud and excited to wake up each morning with a syringe ready to go from the night before. Sometimes I'd get too high and pick at my face. Creating and then opening the flesh underneath. While simultaneously shoving bacteria into the skin and then being shocked when it got infected. Needing to spend half the day putting makeup over the wound to go out in public. It was sad and weird and gross and intense. Every moment felt like an elephant was sitting on my chest. The anxiety and pressure of being who I was, was all consuming. I was so wrapped up in the wildness that to sit with someone sober was uncomfortable.

During the rest of the time, I spent hours looking for each one. Since most dealers only specialized in one and, at most, two chemicals. My daily routine became making calls and waiting by the phone, car keys in hand, just in case. It was impossible to judge when an opportunity would arise, so I lived on my dealers' schedule and at the mercy of their requests.

When things were bad, I searched the carpet for hours for any reminiscent of a possible spill. Otherwise, curled up in the fetal position regretting my choices.

Manipulated Memories

The scenario was always the same, inject heroin or my body would shut down, slam meth to wake me up from the heroin, snort Xanax for the anxiety from it. A constant, never-ending cycle.

Let me note here that there were many circumstances and events that I have not added into this story. I am giving you a synopsis from my perspective. And doing the best I can to remember the timeline. I moved back and forth all over this country so many times it would be ridiculous to keep saying it. I'm a Gemini and running around came naturally.

Yearning for sobriety again around 2015 I made my way back to Southern California, and into another addiction program with no way to know I would re-meet Damien there. The project leaders had spiritually connected us and it was about to be our world war moment.

After another thirty days of inpatient treatment at the hospital I decided that this time I would try and take my recovery more seriously. I'd heard about a residential community where veterans could live together, take classes and get resources that weren't available in sober living homes. It was known as the hardest program in the city, and I needed more help than I could get anywhere else.

Veterans Village of San Diego (VVSD) was impressive. It housed up to a hundred and thirty vets with apartment style rooms with bunkbeds and a bathroom. But it was regimented like the military, forcing structure and rules to live by. We had classes all day and strict curfews and programming that kept us busy at night. The ratio of men to women was staggering with a hundred plus to thirteen. So, I stuck out like a sore thumb. And although getting attention was a subconscious need, I didn't like that I couldn't blend in. The moment I stepped into any facility like that, something in me changes. I follow the rules and play the good kid. Going above and beyond to be the best student. I didn't do it on purpose, but it ruffled feathers along the way.

I made it four months this time before being ready to rejoin society. I left the program with a new car, a pocket full of cash, and the slightest bit of hope. At the time, I'd been dating a guy from treatment who came to live with me, in the living room of an apartment in La Jolla. We will call him Todd. He was a tatted-up skateboarder type who made me laugh constantly.

I felt inspired to try something new, so I registered for a make-up artistry class at The Bellus Academy. It was a skill I picked up naturally and wanted to learn more about. My self-sabotaging characteristics came with, and I used drugs throughout the course. Then found myself too intoxicated to attend the final. One exam away and never went back. A pattern of my lack of follow-through in times of immense importance. I'd get one step away from finishing something that promised a better life.

My relationship with Todd ended and I moved into Jera's guest house apartment when she moved home. Within a couple months I didn't have to pay rent anymore since the owner was losing the house. I signed up for the Esthetician course at the same school and began to have a large income from the G.I Bill, for someone like me. Without many bills meant I had more than enough to pay for my drug habit.

The guesthouse was perfect for me but filled with the leftover junk Jera didn't want to take with her back to Washington. Dirty clothes, cat and dog piss in the bedroom had me sleeping on the couch in the living room, instead of cleaning it up.

When she was there the place was filled with animals, and when she left, it still smelled that way. I cleaned up the living room although there was no hope for the boxes and random old T.V that sat in the middle. The backyard was disgusting with old chew toys and feces everywhere, couches and tools that didn't make the trip, covered with tarps that didn't hide much. I avoided all except the bathroom and kitchen that I passed on the way to my bed. It was gross and I didn't care, because it was mine. The lady next door was the best, willing to give me a couple of Percocet's if I was too sick to go to school. She should've been handed my certificate because without her I wouldn't have graduated.

Jera had been dating Phill for around nine years at this point. She went back to school and became a veterinarian assistant, which made us all proud and made a lot of sense. Phill was a person whose relationship with her, and I were very different, but equally toxic. He was hilarious and I giggled constantly when he was around, and I could sense it drove Jera up the wall, but I couldn't help it. She barely smiled let alone laughed.

Manipulated Memories

I'm not saying we didn't have fun, because we did. But that's all we had, that seemed to be all I was good for. And I was crushed about it. I wanted her to be my best friend. The person I told everything to.

I saw other sisters have a special bond. A secret language that even their parents didn't understand. But we were never that. If we were a cartoon, I'd be drawn physically holding her skirt hem, being thrown around as she stomped through life with a big Dorito on her shoulder. Holding a sign that said, "I took care of her, and now she won't go away." Since she was fourteen months older, she convinced herself she raised me. Which is impossible because she was in diapers at the same time as me, but she still believes it. She did wake me up for school, but not because she was responsible, it was because she liked life. She was beautiful so it was different for her. I lived in her hand-me-down clothes, and everything else.

There was no way around the fact that Jera was the favorite, and that gave her a little pep in her step. I didn't have the same relationship with life. I never did get to get out from under her, and this book won't be the day that happens. Just one more reason for them to disown someone they never claimed anyway. Like anyone you spend a lot of time with, we knew each other. At least she knew what I allowed her to know. All three of us partied like there was no tomorrow and fought like it to. It's just that when that happened, I didn't have anyone to defend me. Phill took her side; our parents took her side, and our siblings stayed out of it. Even if Jera was wrong, all because I didn't have a leg to stand on and wasn't accomplished enough to get one.

I don't want to give the impression that we NEVER got along, that's simply untrue. It lasted about three days; every time we saw each other. Filled with drugs, drinking and dance clubs. There was no intimate anything, no deep discussions, no reminiscing on the sad upbringing and no dreams other than hers, about the future. I couldn't tell her about the intense stuff I'd been through because I was ashamed. I didn't want to be known for that. I was already behind the standards of society; I couldn't take having her look at me like I was pathetic. Not anymore than she already did. To be fair they didn't know if I was gonna be alive to have a future anyway, and to be honest neither did I.

Phill and Jera broke up some weeks before I moved into the apartment, and she met and left town with another man. Someone I didn't have much time to get to know but he seemed nice enough. Even though as her sister I only heard the bad stuff. She ended up pregnant a few months after, and because I was in school, and on drugs, I couldn't go visit and she resented me for that too, and I couldn't blame her.

In my loneliness in between studying and class, I put a message on Facebook that I was looking for new friends and Damien replied right away with, "I will be your friend." I thought it was sweet and had always thought he was sexy, so we texted back and forth. It was innocent at first, and we decided to meet even though I was honest and unapologetic about my drug use.

Manipulated Memories

He invited himself over to hang out, and I tried to tidy up my unkempt apartment, but it was a gruesome mess. When he got there, I could see by the look on his face that he wasn't impressed. Still when he walked in, I was helpless to his charm, falling in love instantly, which is never a good idea. Hopelessly infatuated by his Hispanic complexion and abnormally high sex drive. The red flags were everywhere, but I chose to ignore 'em.

While first dating, I finished the Esthetics trade school program but didn't stop using drugs, barely making it through the course. We acted like college kids, utterly obsessed with each other. It was clear my heart was his, and he knew it. But my intuition tried to tell me there was something I was missing. Trying to warn me that his intentions weren't good.

I couldn't have known it but he resented the attention I received at VVSD, and behind the scenes, his goal was to knock me down a peg. To prove I didn't deserve the praise I got. He thought I was wasting my good looks and had become an embarrassment. So his friends made a bet that he could make me fall in love and then destroy my life. An idea that he thought he had come up with on his own but had been set up years before. He didn't know that there was a bigger picture that needed to get sorted out. A picture that had many people involved over decades. Where the goal was to destroy us all. We all walked straight into the spider's web.

The sex demon inside him festered and had him dancing with the devil. The programming he didn't know he'd had, guided him towards the dark web, and a deviant urge to push the limits of reality in different ways, giving him permission to live a provocative sex addicted lifestyle. Filled with fantasies and then acts beyond most people's wildest dreams. His abusive personality was cultivated since he was a child, and although he was intense, I ask you to consider that when making a judgment. He wasn't in control of his thoughts, and the anger he felt didn't have a way of expressing itself. The trauma of his training in the program, oversees deployment and bruises on his heart from lack of love, compounded over time. The Mk-ultra stuff sat in the back of his mind just waiting to destroy him. A ticking time bomb was set to detonate when he met me.

I often wish someone had taught me about personality disorders in school, but I found out the hard way that Damien was narcissistic, and I was painfully empathic. And since I people pleased my way through life, convinced I had very little value at all, I needed someone to wake me up from that illusion. The incorrect assumption that I could skirt by receiving as little as possible from the undeserving people I put on a pedestal. Anyone including him who gave me any attention at all, were worshipped like gods, with massages and gifts.

I called and asked how his day was every day. Invested in his emotional wellbeing and spent hours listening to his story. Taking on his sad and angry demons like they were my own. I coddled him and his wild behavior and walked on the eggshells he created. It was tense and chaotic even in the beginning, but I thrived on it, needed it even, to feel comfortable. It was all I knew.

Two people couldn't be more opposite. If he wasn't angry, he was quiet, plain and reserved, almost childlike. More often than not wearing superhero graphic tees. Cultivating his outward appearance to seem unassuming, but his contempt for life was obvious. I was rowdy, adventure seeking, and oblivious. But I fell in love with the idea of a savior. I didn't see the writing on the wall that he was never who I thought he was.

Around the same time, money started going missing from my purse and bank account, but I was too scared and unsure of myself to bring it up. Sometimes I wouldn't remember days, and things weren't adding up around him either. I was confused and yet unable to tell anyone. Once he told me about his sex addiction, saying that he found a way to ease his pain from life without getting sick. Claiming he needed his body to defend himself. It didn't take long for me to catch on. My energy sensitive nature meant I could feel it whenever he slept with someone else. My heart chakra would pulse and itch, warning me of trouble.

Graduating the Esthetics program should've been a steppingstone in the right direction, but I wasn't ready to grow up. I was smack dab in the middle of my Saturn return and about to be shown how much it'd take for me to change my ways. Slowly I watched as Damien changed his demeanor, from wanting to help and caring for me when sick, into being volatile with sparks of violence. He groomed me into a toy he could play with when he wanted to, and discard when he didn't. His sharp tongue convinced me I needed him, and that no one else could love a person like me.

Clues about his depravities showed up as hairs that didn't match mine and random clothing were found inside his apartment and car. I was so distraught about it I started wearing them around the house, displaying his infidelity. Trying to convince myself it didn't bother me. He'd shake his head and look at the ground in embarrassment and tell me to take them off. Saying they were his cousins I conveniently never met.

When I think back, this was more disturbing than I'd originally imagined. I was no more than a hundred pounds at that point and being 5 ft tall meant I could buy my clothes in the children's section. So, whose clothes were they?

Over time, I could no longer have friends or visit my family. Everything in my world became about hiding how terrible he was to me. Damien's a Cancer Sun and Moon, the deeply vengeful, mean and emotionally explosive kind. The best at everything, a man's man when other males were around, and an attention seeking flirt when they weren't. With a baby face that hid it all. He loves his family; I'll give him that. And he is a person who has every reason to be angry with the world. The sad part is, he earned that karma like the rest of us.

He's around five-ten with black hair and tan skin. Naturally, he'd be a slender build, but when we dated, he was a machine with high-velocity workouts and bouts with steroids. Every muscle stuck out defined just enough to make any girl smile, and he knew he was sexy. His unquenchable sexual appetite taught him professional level tools in the bedroom, that he used as weapons. He wore evil tattoos on his chest and arms and angel wings on his shoulder blades. The demons on his body showed up in his big brown eyes. He was twenty-five, and I was thirty, making me feel old, but he said he didn't care.

A typical alpha personality whose sensitive emotional nature didn't match. He learned he needed to protect his soft side and so his shell turned into armor. Very few people have ever seen the person beneath his ego. The kid who didn't get enough love and at the same time got too much attention. His past was riddled with pain, and I can't judge the man he became.

Like the rest of us, the projects separated his mind into multiple characters meant to blindly take orders and not remember. Sometimes I wonder how much of what you'll see in the next few chapters he even knows happened. The side effects of his programming were crushing, he didn't sleep much at all, ever. I was always concerned for his health, but he wouldn't talk about it. Like me, he didn't want to ask for help, and didn't like the meds they tried to put him on, because they numbed his personality. He needed his narcissism to survive, without it he would've been gutted by reality.

Manipulated Memories

Some days, I would come home to either a teenage boy or an infant child, depending on how his day went. And knocking on his door became a roulette game.

To society, he'd seem pretty normal, but he lived a double life as the villain behind closed doors. He did find fistfights more than most with his harsh demeanor and stronger than life ego. It should've been my first clue when his nickname in rehab was Dangerous Damien.

He mentioned he'd been meeting with a group of men in various locations around the US but never told me what for. And sometimes, groups of men would leave his apartment right as I got there, making sure not to introduce themselves. I should've asked a few questions, but he was such a hermit (or so I thought) that I didn't see the need to worry. I was only anxious about him meeting other girls like any other insecure girl would be.

Imagine my surprise when I found out he was part of a secret society of clever boys that got off on hurting people. Using drugs and abusing each other for entertainment. Searching for the most dare devil activities they could find, needing to be close to death to feel alive, and risking themselves to fulfill their dark desires.

One night he left me alone in his apartment while he went to the neighbors to chat, and when the coast was clear of him, I pulled out my paraphernalia and walked into the bathroom. Before I could even open my case of drugs, he slammed the front door open. Smashed into the bathroom and grabbed my stuff. Opening it and throwing my needles and dope outside over the balcony rail and onto the cars below, while screaming. In those instances, I wondered how it was possible he didn't have any shame. Everyone knew what he was doing to me. They heard him breaking stuff and ranting all the time. But he never cared, it didn't faze him, which was fascinating. I didn't put it together until later that he had to have camera's watching me, in order for him to know what I was doing. As we move forward, you'll see why they were there. All the signs were right in front of me, but codependency skewed my vision.

To have his other relationships, he'd fabricate fights between us, to justify his actions. I'd leave after hours of abuse, and his lovers would come over. Some nights he'd follow me when I left, to use my behavior as fuel for the next time I saw him. Most nights I just fled to the V.A. hospital to sleep in my car. Forced to sit alone out of fear that he'd retaliate if I went anywhere else. I'd beg the Creator for someplace safe to go and someone to tell me everything would be okay. I'd cover the windows in my car and hide from the world, using the hospital bathroom to clean up when I could muster the strength. Sometimes waking up in my car foggy and unclear with an internal fear that I couldn't put into words.

Learning later that some nights the project's minions came and took me for my routine evaluations, pulling me from the front seat and carrying me into their car, to check my progress and condition or add new subliminal programming. There was no getting away from them during this period in my life. I didn't think I could handle anymore than I was dealing with anyway, so the universe spared me the details until I was ready.

Some people would call that ignorant naivety, but it was unconscious mental survival. I couldn't spend time focusing on the details of these experiences. I would've gone mad. The best I could do was take each moment as it came and believe that someday it would end.

Damien began recruiting and paying my ex's and his friends, to help him get back at me when I left him. Giving them some sob story about what a terrible person I was. Over and over, I'd leave when he became violent, and the stalking would begin. If I went to a friend's house he didn't like, I'd get assaulted even more when I saw him next. All those people he'd hired would tell him where I was, and sometimes I'd see him following me in a rented car. But my addiction wouldn't let me put together what I already knew was happening.

When I was twenty-two, I got a tattoo on my right side, that says "hidden agenda" in Greek. Until this book, that statement never made sense. When I chose to come to Earth, I knew I was going to have to sacrifice my cherished privacy to be a part of the solution. To stand up for women everywhere who have been told they are worthless, sexually abused or taken advantage of. Show them how to get back up and truly heal the pain by forgiving their perpetrators. Teaching them that they are not victims in the way they think they are. While shining a light on the darkness that creates the need for domination and control in people like this.

I tried to tell Damien about my encounters with being stalked and harassed, but he wouldn't hear it. I thought it bothered him that he couldn't protect me, but he was helping them torture me, and I couldn't see it. He said something profound once about it, "They can't get to you, if you don't let them in." I didn't understand what he meant at the time, but he was right. This wouldn't have happened if I was sober.

He never cared for me the way I thought he did. I've seen his intentions, and I was more of a way to make some cash than anything else. Unbeknownst to me, the video cameras were put there to film everything. The boy's group continuously got bigger by including gym buddies and boys he met online. The more people involved the worse it got for me. They set up a dark web channel where people could watch us, and he'd take donations for suggestions about how he should treat me.

When I looked back at these memories his behaviors made a lot more sense. Like when we had sex and he'd look behind him, which I thought was some strange kink, but he was making it more interesting for the camera. I try my best to have compassion for myself, since I loved him and was too innocent to know better.

One night I woke up to him growling in my face while he thought I was asleep. Standing with one foot on each side of my head, pleasuring himself with an evil grin. I asked what he was doing, and he said, "Just fucking around," enthralled with himself. It was wild but I couldn't keep my eyes open to do anything about it.

I know what I ignored, but I didn't want to fight. I just tried to keep him happy (which was impossible). Attempting to please his five or six times a day sex habit. The thought of him cheating felt more like relief than anything, and it wasn't how I wanted to live, but it became my reality.

I wasn't easy to deal with either. I barely slept or ate, and my emotions were so extreme that I was exploding or emoting all the time. I was jealous because I knew he was sleeping around, but so cowardly that I didn't do anything about it. I obsessed over him to such a degree that it was nauseating for an avoidant attachment style. I watched him turn into a monster, suffocated by me, and to handle it, I used as many drugs as I could get my hands on.

Out of spite, or just to be mean, he called the cops on me a couple times, after abusing me all day. To have some insurance if I tried to tell anyone who he really was. Then he'd cry to me for hours about how sorry he was. We lived like that for years, and I thought about it every day, but didn't know how I was supposed to explain that to people? They'd see the police records and think I did something wrong. Every time the cops came to the apartment, they knew that he was the one doing the abuse, and they tried to get me to tell them the truth, but I wasn't strong enough yet. I thought he'd kill me if I made him look bad, so I ignored their questions, said nothing, and left.

Manipulated Memories

By 2016 I was a full-time student at Massage Therapy school, getting my Holistic Health Practitioners license. But I'd irresponsibly missed a bunch of classes when I didn't feel well or stayed with Damien, because when things were good, we said, I love you, back and forth all day, giggling and laughing while watching our favorite shows. I didn't catch on to the fact that it was all a mirage, but I did start to notice that we never left the house together. The few times we tried to see a movie or go to the beach, he got angry, and we returned. If I looked at someone at all, he'd throw a fit for hours, and he hated that I was bi-sexual, to him, that meant everyone was a threat. Which on some level means he had feelings for me, but it was more like ownership than true love.

The jealousy was so ridiculous that I started to wonder if it was a joke. I didn't know at the time how right I was when I had thoughts like, "Maybe his boyfriends sit around a table and think up ways to torture me, telling him to behave in these insane ways and see how much I will take."

I'm sure these were some of the projects' suggestions poured into his mind or given to him through the internet. Teaching him to be relentless and power hungry, obsessed with control and domination. Playing games with my sanity for profit and enjoyment.

It isn't his fault, but it is his responsibility for what he became. Even though he was taught to be violent and devilish from an early age. Groomed by old Illuminati-type men to be the best predator he could be, and I regret to say he lived up to their expectations.

Manipulated Memories

Feeling unwell got me in trouble for truancy, and my car ended up impounded after I refused to get new tags and insurance for nine months. Now I had to ask him for a ride to school, and although he said it was okay the night before, I knew it wouldn't go well. The deal was that if I were late one more time, I'd be kicked out after seven months into a ten-month program and he knew that.

I woke up on time and got dressed, but Damien wasn't in a generous mood. He rolled out of bed and grumbled, "Fine, let's go." We loaded up the blue ford focus and started off towards my school. I sensed his irritation and predicted the fight he concocted out of nowhere. Fueling a longstanding conflict about how I had previously dated a couple of people he knew. His favorite go-to scenario when he didn't have a real reason to get mad. Before I knew it, he leaned over and smacked me hard in the leg as he was driving. Knowing it was a spot, no one would see. Outrage and fear boiled inside me. I stayed quiet because I had to get there on time. His energy got more aggressive as we got closer to the school. It was eight fifty, and I had to clock in no later than nine. We had just enough time to race into the parking lot, and I could have still made it, but the tone in his voice got louder and louder, and I began to panic. We were blocks from the school now, and my heart filled with joy that we might get there, but he pulled into the parking lot of a store next door, intentionally making me late.

That was the last draw. I did something so far out of my character it scared me. I turned and punched him directly in the nose twice. He spit blood in my face and turned the car around. We drove in silence back to the apartment, where he apologized later, but I would pay for that mistake. Under the anger he seethed, I could sense that he was proud of me in a weird way. He didn't think I'd ever fight back, but he had forced me into a corner for too long and I was done with his shenanigans.

As we laid in bed the next evening, I gently suggested, "You want to watch a movie?" "Sure, I'll find something." It was late, so we snuggled on the mattress that sat directly on the floor, in his studio apartment in the not-so-good part of town. With only enough room for a small lounge chair, desk and T.V stand. We both complained that it was hot that night, but we're too cheap to buy another fan. Half empty soda bottles filled with cigarette butts leaned next to the bed, and the entire place smelled like sex and weed. A proper bachelor pad that never saw a mop or duster. The cabinets were stained, and the counters were wiped but still dirty. The bars on the windows behind the toilet gave it character, he told himself, and the crusty blinds barely held back the light during the day.

It wasn't much but it was the first place we had where we could be alone together. At first it felt safe and exciting. We were free to be ourselves finally, and I found out early on that that wasn't all it was cracked up to be. When the mask he shared with the world came off, I was in for a rude awakening. His place became a temporary prison every time I came over, and although every day wasn't terrible, most days were, and that would turn into all very soon.

Bang, bang, an urgent knock hit the front door. Damien jumped up quickly, "Who the fuck is that!?" I curled up, nervous for someone to see me without makeup on. A female's voice whispered while giggling, and from the opened door, I heard her say, "Can I see her?" He walked back inside smiling and shut and locked the door. My suspicion was raised, and I asked who it was, but his response was meaningless. "Just some drunk girl who lives in the building. Don't worry about it." He offered me a drink of Gatorade to shut me up, which was out of character, and I passed out immediately.

It was late the next morning when I came to, my mind foggy and eyelids heavy. Fear surrounded me as the sensations in my backside told me I'd spent the night raped in the most savage way (punishment for hitting him). Damien grabbed me around the head and shoulders, visibly shaking. "Are you alright? he asked with sadness in his tone. "Ya, I'm alright," I replied nonchalantly. He kissed me all over the face and told me how much he loved me, guilt oozing from his pores. I pulled back and announced I needed to use the bathroom. "Go ahead," he said with a giddy smile. Like he couldn't believe I was alive at all. On the way to the washroom, each step was unbearable. I could feel the scratching back and forth of ripped skin around a gaping hole stretched beyond its limits. Just another day in the presence of a monster, I said to myself, knowing I wouldn't tell anyone. I was forced to have another pep talk with my reflection while standing on my tippy toes. "I don't want to fight with him all day, so let's act like this never happened. I don't have the energy." When I made it back to the living room, he was crying but silent, wiping tears from his face, he grabbed me by the arm, forcing me to cuddle.

Throughout the three-and-a-half-year on and off again joke of a relationship, I woke up four times, knowing he'd raped me while asleep. Unable to ignore the pain in my backside, which we never used. I downplayed the experience and said to myself, "Hmmm, that's strange," and let it go, because I couldn't handle processing such a sad reality. My brain was set to fawn the people who harmed me, so in some way, each trauma with him made us closer.

These were the only times I noticed, but he'd done it every time I did something he didn't like. I wouldn't have noticed if he hadn't gone that far. We had sex so much that I was always in pain otherwise. I told myself he was acting out his gay fantasies and would be ashamed if I brought it up. His hysteric fits when someone even suggested he could be homosexual already had me question his sexuality, but there were many other signs. I could only imagine what he'd act like if I embarrassed him, and I didn't want to find out.

After another fight, and me ending the relationship again, I ran off and stayed with my best friend Erin for a while. Attempting to take some outpatient addiction classes at the hospital, but that didn't last long. I was chronically heartbroken, and it showed. Desperately doing whatever I could to stay busy, because my Gemini mind needed distraction. Most days were spent at the Methadone clinic or looking for drugs. I was malnourished, emotionally disturbed and angry I'd let myself go through these things. Clearly slipping into the abyss. Eventually, the paranoia became relentless, and I was near breaking. So, I checked myself into the hospital for a doctor's review, knowing that something terrible would happen if I continued that way.

Chapter 13

Hell is empty and all the devils are here.
~ William Shakespeare

I wandered into the hospital defeated, looking like a skeleton. My arms pincushions, and my body sick and mentally exhausted. After I expressed what I was going through at home, they decided they'd put me in the mental ward. Sitting in an exam room, I waited to be brought upstairs when I fell asleep.

As I opened my eyes, I saw I was laid on a hospital bed in a dark room with my legs spread into stirrups. Surrounded by what I can only describe as male Satanists in black robes. They laughed and taunted me while chanting words and circling me. One brushed the hair off my face and hovered next to my ear, whispering, "We are going to remove your I.U.D and replace it with one that will kill you. You won't remember this, and you'll finally be gone forever. We've been waiting for you. Your innocence kept you alive, but we're finishing the deal today. You thought you got away scot-free (laughing). We wanted you to believe that. But, truthfully, you're a puppet to a system you don't understand, and we will show you the power of Satan."

Manipulated Memories

The doctor, using a small light, removed my I.U.D and grabbed a new one with tongs. He held it over a tray and another man poured a liquid on top. In unison, they all began to dance and speak in Latin. In rhythm, they took turns poking and berating me. The energy created from their jumping around and dancing movements seemed to power some kind of spell. All I could do was cry in horror silently, watching the doctor's facial features, as he appeared troubled. Intuitively understanding he was forced to be there. As his hands shook, he was reminded several times to hurry up. A pen-like device was held to my face, and a bright light hit my eyes, as the rest of the men covered theirs.

I woke up startled but safe in the mental ward, believing the sensations in my privates were from being sexually assaulted. Everything was blurry and tears fell down my face without reason. Grabbing my knees to my chest in the fetal position, I rocked back and forth, saying to myself, "Something's wrong."

As I laid there, trying to ignore my harsh existence, a spirit grabbed my astral body removing me from my flesh suit, and pulled me quickly upwards. I flew through the building and hovered in mid-air above the roof. Looking down to see the hospital swarming with evil beings, like in the Constantine movie. Thousands of them crawling over the entire complex. Through the darkness, I could see four dots of glowing gold light, and sensed there were people protecting as many of us as they could. When I was abruptly dropped back into my body without seeing who had abducted me.

Manipulated Memories

For some reason, it didn't scare me, but did give me a new perspective, and solidified what I already knew. That the hospital I was in was infested, and I needed to get out. I lost my love of California rather quickly.

Even though I kept having these paranormal experiences, they were so different from my perceived reality that I didn't think about it. Almost like they were only meant to soothe me in the moment. And because there was so much danger in my life, my brain didn't have room to think about anything out of its control. I needed the bandwidth I had to find ways to survive.

To the outside world, it looked like my mind was swimming with paranoid symptoms. So, the doctors kept giving me more medications, which only hindered my ability to figure out the truth. Until then I couldn't address the fact that I was shattered from the inside, with little hope for the future. To be fair, they didn't know what they didn't know.

After around a month I was released from the hospital, oblivious to what'd really happened there. I still wanted to be sober, so I enrolled back into VVSD after another thirty days in the inpatient treatment. Again, Damien pursued me aggressively, visiting and promising he'd changed. Although I knew he wasn't good for me, my obsession and programming kept me a lovesick puppy, addicted to the drama, convinced he was the only person who could save me.

Eventually, he asked me to leave and come live with him full time. But it'd only been a few months since the lady I lived with lost the house, and I was rightfully skeptical, knowing I'd have to take my belongings to his place. I did it anyway, packing up everything I owned and trucking it up to his house then tossing the bags on the floor. We played nice for a couple days and I genuinely thought we could coexist.

After another fight, I returned the next day, and everything of mine was gone. As I walked into the house, Damien was lying on the bed with tears running down his face. I demanded to know what happened, "Where's all my stuff? He could barely speak. "I got mad and threw it away, I'm so sorry," he tumbled over his words, rocking back and forth, holding his knees, begging me not to leave him. Hitting himself in the head while repeating how sorry he was. Tears welled up in my eyes as I believed he was in pain. "I had to see if you loved me," he sobbed. In a less harsh tone than the situation demanded I asked him, "What does that even mean, Damien?" He repeated himself again and again, still rocking. "I will buy you new stuff, I'm so sorry."

When I watched the reenactment of him and his friends ransacking my stuff, I realized they were laughing and enjoying themselves. Then I learned that Damien wouldn't replace my things within a couple of days. One time, he did take me to a thrift shop to get a few things but threw it away again. He was making a fool of me, and it became obvious.

I got an uber to Erin's where a smell of deception was in the air, and spirit has since shown me a walk-in soul had replaced him just before this. Just like I came to help the human in this body, someone came to harm me in his. I noticed right away that the way he spoke and how he was acting was out of character. He argued with me for no reason, and I felt uncomfortable from the drugs we did that seemed off. Unsettled, I walked to the store less than a block away to cool off and figure out what the heck was going on.

When four Spanish looking men pulled up next to a freight truck, got out and slowly closed in on me from all four directions. I ran into the gas station and used their phone to call a cab, begging him to let me stay in the store until it got there. As we drove up the I805 to La Jolla, I saw three cars, plus the freight truck, following us. After making it into the E.R, I thought I was safe.

But the moment I stepped into the building; I got a horrible feeling in my stomach. Danger set off my internal alarm as I sat in the exam room, trying to remind me of what happened the last time. When a voice inside me yelled, "RUN!" Jumping up, I ran out of the room and into the police station of the hospital in my gown. Screaming that someone was going to hurt me, looking crazy as ever. A cop came out of his office and took me by the arm, thrashing and screaming. Dragging me back to the room I was in and standing guard with the staff while they injected something in me to knock me out. This was the moment when I figured out, I was in way over my head.

Suddenly my fuzzy eyes opened, and I was in the back of the freight truck moving on what felt like a freeway. Turning my head to the left, I saw I was hooked to an I.V bag and heart monitor. Further to my left were three girls in gowns and a nurse in front of each of us. My memory went blank as

Manipulated Memories

I disassociated from the experience. I came back while inside a Scarface style giant mansion with open areas as far as the eye could see. Spanish men filled the space. I was standing in the center of a room without the I.V in, being told to dance, but I could hardly move. I got the feeling we were being used as spectacles for entertainment, but I couldn't speak. I left my body again. My next memory was sitting on a couch on top of an obese man naked, while he smoked a cigar, the smell repulsed my senses. I felt emotionally blank, without pain or anxiety. Sitting lifeless trying to sift through the confusion, but I couldn't handle what was happening and I released myself again. Only to awaken huddled on an unknown floor naked, holding my knees with my arms in an unknown building. With walls made of cement and wood boards barely hanging on, pop marked with holes covered by plastic bags and tarps. It stunk like animals and was so cold I could see my breath.

I rocked back and forth as a group of men circled me laughing. One man stepped back and picked up a bucket, thrashing it in my direction. Covering my face, head, and neck with ice-cold water. I focused on my breathing, doing everything I could not to hyperventilate. My heart pounded in my chest, and I begged to go home. More than once in my life, I would've welcomed death; this was one of them. I tried to move back, but the chain around my left ankle held me to a rod bolted to the ground. The concrete was freezing, but I was too weak to get up. My teeth chattered with fear as I played out every possible scenario that could come after this.

Manipulated Memories

Would I die right here in the middle of nowhere? Would anyone notice if I went missing?

I thought I could hear giggling behind the door and chatter about a party. "A show in my honor," they said, laughing. Each person who came through the door spoke to me like a dog, ordering me around, prodding at my humanity. Someone dried me with towels and dressed me in something sexy. They teased me with riddles and promises of gentleness while eyeing each other and smiling. Telling me not to fear, but I knew they were lying. They wanted me to fear them; they got off on it. To those kinds of people, fear is a drug.

Tears dripped down my face, and I tried to hide them by looking down. Damien grabbed my face and pulled it towards him. He licked my tears and said, "Salty, I love 'em." Was this real? Was my ex-boyfriend standing over me with evil on his face? How did he know these people? Was he responsible for getting me here? My head swam with questions, but I could tell he wouldn't be answering them.

I concentrated on my left ear nearest the door. To hear the rustling of the people gathering and the sound of voices from all directions. Music began to play, and I heard someone introducing tonight's events on a loudspeaker. Unable to make out what they said over the sound of the crowd cheering, I was left alone to wait and pray for help I knew wasn't coming.

Without warning, a satanic ceremony began with Latin incantations broadcasted over a microphone. Someone suddenly opened the door and grabbed me by the arm.

Manipulated Memories

Physically forcing me through a corridor into the focal point of the large building with dirt floors. The room was dark, sprinkled with men and women wearing black robes. Candles lit the peripheral, and a spotlight aimed toward the middle. In the center was a boxing ring, with a hundred or so people encircling it.

Two girls in strippers' outfits paraded around holding signs with numbers. They danced, did cartwheels and dry humped the air. Distinctive females, opposite looking but both gorgeous and deadly. One exotic with tan skin and long dark hair, possibly one of the most beautiful creatures I'd ever seen. The other, had long blonde hair and light eyes. A master at seduction, twirling around the stage like a nearly naked ballerina. Every man couldn't help but lust after her.

Shocked at this intensity, I froze. I could hear and see the terror, but I felt completely numb. I watched as my body trembled uncontrollably. I allowed my tears to flow, so petrified I didn't notice. They lead me into the crowd, through a group of people who parted as we walked past. Everyone knew the deal, and this was not their first rodeo. There were special tickets to this sort of thing that people planned for all year. The crowd had a ten to one ratio men to women. Everyone excited by something different.

I was only one of the four girls meant for the stage that night, and it was show time. As we got closer to the net, I saw a group of men grab something white and turn around. In unison they put on masks that look like the V for vendetta character, and I thought to myself, "I wish I'd watched that movie; maybe then I could get the joke." Later I put together that Damien had the same one sitting on the TV stand at his house in Florida, just to taunt me.

One man hoisted me up to stand on the top of the ring, outside the ropes. While another came over from the center and lifted me inside. The crowd went wild, cheers, laughter and growling all at the same time. I noticed a rumble of energy, something like a dark thunder of thirst for wickedness. I could feel that those people had waited for this for a long time, and they'd be getting something for their money. It wasn't just about sex and torture but domination and savagery.

The spotlight shined from above directly into my eyes...and my heart sank. From the corner of my sight, I saw shapes tided to each of the four corner poles. Ropes connected in the center to a sex swing. One that straps your feet in to be able to turn a person upside down. A man attempted to walk me towards it, but I couldn't get my feet to move. I scanned the arena for an escape route, but it was hopeless, that seat was my destiny.

Instinctively, I struggled and flailed my arms screaming, which only enticed the crowd. They snickered and hissed with excitement. I was forced into the chair on my back, legs fully spread into the wide stirrups, arms attached to ropes above and behind me. My breath felt shallow and weighted. I looked around the room searching for one good soul, one decent person to help me out of the nightmare. But I was met with darkness shining brightly in everyone's eyes, from the Adrenochrome being peddled there.

Around the outside of the ring, I saw seven or eight men, playing with the masks on their faces, making a point to terrify me. One by one, they started kissing each other and taking off their clothes. Dancing like strippers to get the crowd ready for more. They each slowly made their way towards me, showing off their flexibility and stamina by jumping around the ring. As the first person made it to the center, I closed my eyes. Deciding that if I was going through this, I didn't want to see anything.

Intuitively I could sense that Jordan sat in a chair next to the ring, his head down. I didn't know him consciously yet, and he was trying desperately to get ahold of his extremely intoxicated partner who was acting a fool. Embarrassed and ashamed of the fiasco but still watching as they ravaged me.

When a cold object ran gently down my stomach and back up around my neck. I didn't have to open my eyes to know it was a knife. The adrenaline kicked into my system, and I had trouble keeping my eyes closed. The room was spinning, and I was swimming in fear. My breath quickened, and I prayed to myself silently. "Creator, if you can hear me, don't let me die like this." Another man got between my legs and stimulated me. Together they made howling noises, signaling to begin their feast. I started to feel nauseous and complained to deaf ears.

Each caressed me sweetly, confusing my mind, getting deeper and stronger with each movement. I wanted to throw up, but my body's chemicals were rushing. If there was a more paradoxical position to be in, I couldn't think of it.

My body disobeyed me, and I couldn't help but be aroused by the pleasure. Each person took a turn forcing me to orgasm, and the place erupted each time. I gave up and laid as still as I could, staring off into the corner of the stadium, allowing what would be, to be. Noticing the hardening of my heart with every thrust. I hid inside myself and took my consciousness somewhere else while my body was defiled. My heart broke into pieces as each one took their turn. In every unimaginable way, they tore at my soul. I had no rational sense of time, but the first-round buzzer sounded within the hour, and I thought I was done for.

Cl...thud...cl...thud...cl...thud...cl...thud.

The sounds echoed across the ceiling, as something walked in from the back. Heavy and muscular noises reverberated off the walls. Strong breathing got closer and closer, and a smell I recognized punctured the air. As the donkey stepped up to the ring, I could feel its hooves bashing on the ground, as it was led up a ramp I hadn't seen before. The ropes were moved out of the way, and the giant mammal met me in the center. The audience went wild with anticipation, and I laughed at the insanity. Was I in a lousy movie role and did not get the memo? Did things like this really happen?

The terror was so uncomfortable it made my etheric body jump out of my skin. The ringleaders jumped around ruthlessly, aroused by the legions of dark beings that filled the building, drunk and tameless. The truth, my friends,

Manipulated Memories

about people like this, is that they are everywhere. They're your friends, lovers, and business partners. They run our government, and they "serve and protect." They pass laws and give sentences right before they buy their tickets.

The next thing I knew, I was walking back to the freight truck. As I shuffled up the ramp a nurse handed me two brand-new name-brand outfits and a pair of shoes. I still remember the smell of them. I felt like a person again, grateful and thankful, almost like it was a job, and I was being rewarded. They ruined that moment by hooking me back up to an I.V and telling me to hold the drip bag stand, in a rude tone.

The nurses laughed at us on the way home, acting annoyed when they had to tend to us. Telepathically I heard their every thought. Fantasizing about the money they'd made and what they'd do with it. Vacations to exotic places and cars they planned to buy. It was a brutal, dark, inhumane conversation to listen to. Something out of a bad movie, and I thought the entire world was disturbed. One nurse, named Jennifer, had a sad look in her eyes, I could sense how guilty she felt. I watched her most of the trip home and fell asleep sometime afterwards.

The next day I woke up back in the mental ward, although this time, I remembered most of what happened. My body reeked of cigars and liquor, my hair was ratted, and my privates throbbed.

Fear of being in the hospital engulfed me. I figured out that I wasn't the only one who knew what was going on, and another girl and I would talk about it in code, scared someone would hear us. After a couple days we got a new patient on the floor, who poked and prodded for information about the 'sex trafficking happening in the basement.' He was a spy, looking to see how much we knew by asking pointed questions to see if we'd talk, but no one did. We weren't that stupid.

Over time, I saw them do it to at least four other girls. Always on a Friday. They'd wake up with glass in their hair, smelling of cigarettes, questioning themselves, but none of us had the balls to say it. They didn't remember anyway. Eventually, I asked the other girl who knew what was up, how she ended up there? Her answer sent chills throughout my entire body. "They came and took me from my apartment." This caused a sickening fear to rise inside me. Would they come to get me anywhere? How do I stop this from happening again? And who were these people?

My memory couldn't allow me to remember Damiens involvement because the weight of it would have killed me. So, I went along my life believing it was some random Spanish men in a big fancy house. Thankfully my obliviousness didn't hold on too hard to the facts of what that most likely meant. I couldn't handle another ounce of anxiety, no matter how real the danger was. I was hardly functioning as it was. My mind was such a champion to keep me able to put one foot in front of the other at this point. To think anything it did was wrong would be lunacy. We are powerful creatures, and my power was shown by the amount of precariousness I escaped from.

Manipulated Memories

The nurse from the truck Jennifer, found me walking the halls one day, and pulled me aside, "You need to get out of here," she whispered in my ear. The worried look on her face said she wasn't kidding, and I was surprised she even risked talking to me at all. I shook my head in agreement and began to beg my therapist to transfer me to a treatment program anywhere but California. The only one available was in Cleveland, OH. The bed wasn't available for a few days after I got released, so I planned to go to Damien's until it was time. Although my intuition knew better.

Apparently, the lure of money was too great for doctors and nurses so close to the Mexico border. It enticed even good people into diabolical human trafficking rings. A trade I knew happened in other countries worldwide but nothing I considered in my wildest nightmares here in the U.S. They were running a perfect system by taking young drug addicted girls for a night, because no one would notice. Then throw them in the looney bin. Who'd care anyway?

The meds they gave us were likely a benzodiazepine or something like it. Which kept us coherent enough but gave most amnesia. I know for sure; they were counting on me to forget. But they didn't consider that Damien had been drugging me already for years, which meant they didn't give me enough. This revelation put an enormous price tag on my head.

Now there was more than one group that wanted me gone, and the threat lingered in the air around me. From the dangerous collections of people, I couldn't hide from, and the police that either knowingly or unknowingly helped them sell us.

Thirty days after walking the short hallway of the hospital doing nothing, and since he kept showing up for visits, I was released to Damien. President Trump got elected while I was there, and I was convinced the entire world had gone mad. Even though I could care less about politics.

Since I had just gotten kicked out of school I didn't know if my G.I Bill money would be there when I left the hospital. But that's how the universe proves itself to me every time. By being there even when it has no reason to be. I was saved by that cash in my account in many ways.

When walking out of the hospital I felt an instant relief, like I'd just won the lottery. I couldn't believe I'd survived whatever that was. "Somebody has to tell someone about this!" Then with an internal eyeroll, "I'd hate to be that girl," while nervously chuckling. But something in me knew this was only the beginning. That I remembered what happened for a reason. To be a loudspeaker for this kind of thing. But right now, I wasn't in good shape and even the thought of that I couldn't handle. Never in a billion years did I fathom talking about this or standing up for myself and the other girls. At this time, I was scared for my life, and rightfully so. At that moment, I wanted to hide far away, and for as long as possible. I didn't know if I'd ever feel safe again.

I only had a few days before I was off to treatment, so I thought I'd hang out with Damien, but he was acting even more strange than usual. He got bedbugs while I was gone and had a meltdown about it. I was pushed past my breaking point with his tantrum and finally left him for good. I got on a bus heading back home, less sad than I thought I'd be. Grateful he was out of my life. Not even tempted to answer any one of his hundred phone calls. I was free.

Chapter 14

Walls have ears.
Doors have eyes.
Trees have voices.
Beasts tell lies.
Beware the rain.
Beware the snow.
Beware the man you think you know.
~Catherine Fisher

When I showed up, the Cleveland treatment center announced, "Don't walk two blocks in either direction without a buddy." If that doesn't set the stage, I'm unsure what would. Right away, I started talking to doctors and therapists about the six months I spent mentally trapped in California with Tiny. The look on their faces was painful and they always said the same thing, "I'm so sorry that happened to you." I didn't like that the support around me gave me more reason to feel self-pity, it pissed me off.

Manipulated Memories

Within the first week, I learned about the center's art classes and signed up immediately. The first time I walked into the studio revived my passion for creating. Something about a room full of brushes and canvases fed my starving soul. The lively teacher announced, "Make whatever you want," no stipulations or requirements. Allowing me to do anything I wanted made me as happy as I could possibly be, given the circumstances. It inspired and drove what little faith I had left in the world.

After graduating, I went back to Washington State where most of my family had migrated to the same town I lived with my dad in. Mostly because of its cheap cost of living. To set up a new life of masking my feelings the best I could, with working out and starting a new job.

Jera had given birth to my nephew Daltin around six months before I got there, and he taught me what unconditional love was the moment I held him. His tiny hands and loving Pisces spirit were the most precious things I'd ever encountered. I wanted to spend every second I could with him and would've, had she let me. Watching him grow up was some of the happiest moments of my life, and we had a special bond that I'll never have with anyone else. He was born on leap day which means he'll be an important person to this world. Someday he'll create change here in his own way.

Now that I was back around the family, I was forced to see the remnants of the over $100,000 my mom had given Jera to "Help with Daltin." Now I'm not stupid, I know kids cost a lot of money, but the new car she bought was less than child friendly, and where the rest went...I couldn't tell ya. Some toys, a crib and clothes didn't cost anyone that kind of money and I was bitter. My mom still refused to give me anything. It was like something was keeping her from treating me like the rest of my siblings. Kayla got a new car at the same time, right after my mom's last husband died.

This time would end up being the heartbreak of my life, when I was first kept away and then banned from seeing Daltin, after I started using again. Jera started employing him as a bargaining tool and a way to hurt me. She knew no matter what I was doing with my life I would've done anything to protect him. He was the best thing that'd ever happened to me, and she hated it. She was jealous that we were so close, because she was so cut off from her emotions she couldn't be. But someday, when he's older, he'll learn about me, and it'll be up to him what he wants to do. Until then I think of him often, sending him love. Knowing the family he's being raised in will force him to be strong.

My resentment towards my family kept growing, although I didn't have a voice to say it. I'm not saying they should've given me a bunch of money, but why not a car or some clothes? Maybe put something away so I could've used it when I got sober. I was more pissed that they didn't even consider that. My Dad made me feel bad that I cared about the money at all. Like I wasn't supposed to notice, probably because he'd been giving Jera money for years and had his own guilt to bear.

Too bad they didn't know that Jera was buying drugs with it the entire time. I didn't say anything because sometimes she shared it with me. My poor family believed in her, just as much as I did. She played us all.

No matter what I did during the day, the dreams would come, and I'd spend my nights haunted by Tiny. He lurked in my thoughts and lived in my flashbacks. Certain smells made me cringe, and the feelings of disgust would flood in. I was caught in the thought pattern that he wouldn't have happened if I'd been sober. The same words Jera said to me, had become how I saw everything, and the blaming of myself threw me into another spiral.

No one ever put together what I was going through, even though on more than one occasion, I tried telling someone in the family. They all responded the same way. "You shouldn't have been there and need to get over it." They failed to see that by enabling me to act like it didn't happen, meant I couldn't heal from it.

Even though I was on my own and left to my own devices, life improved for a while. I hated that I couldn't get away from the nagging feeling that I had a deeper purpose to my life. Sometimes I questioned what it could be. Did I remember what transpired at the hospital for a reason? Or would I just ruin things more for myself by coming forward. It wasn't clear what I was supposed to do. Just an inner knowing that I was meant for greatness. I refused to give up no matter how bad I kept messing things up.

Manipulated Memories

I made it about five months in my new apartment before returning to drugs. It was an up and down time for me with it. If Jera and I were on good terms I could get away with getting high sometimes, because she would tell the family I was okay. But if me and her had it out over something, the entire family would step to her side and look at me like scum. I didn't realize that she was already the matriarch of the family.

By now, my personality had changed entirely, and I couldn't feel anything except anger that I had to keep it together when I felt dead inside. I didn't last long working at Dick's Sporting goods after I got t-boned on my way home from work, a block from my apartment. I was once again defeated by the shit storm of a life I was having, and without using any of the coping techniques I'd been taught, I was a mess again.

Naturally, I ended up back in the hospital. Where they offered me another treatment program in a couple weeks. Every time I had to go back, felt like a failure. Like I couldn't handle being human and everyone else could. I wish I'd given myself more grace and compassion, at least I never gave up. Damien came to visit that same week while I waited to go, which was the first time he met my mother. We weren't back together but I was lonely. He played nice and acted like a victim, talking about how crazy I was, saying he only wanted to help. Complete hogwash.

Those two got along great, so great in fact, they'd had sex, while I was detoxing in the other room. I only learned about that many years later, but it wasn't the first time my mom had been implicated in that kind of drama. Although with Jera's ex Phill we didn't have proof. Now that I've seen her with Damien, I can almost guarantee she'd had them both.

My money for school showed up again (which I would end up paying all back) and we started staying at hotels in the area, trying not to bother my mom…which I'm not sure was fair since she was staying in my apartment. I of course got high all day, and Damien stole some of my xanex when I was in the bathroom. I searched everywhere, like a wild person. Overturning my car and stumped at what could've possibly happened. I never saw him take drugs, so I didn't even consider that he might. A couple times it was obvious he had done something, just never with me. He watched me scrounge around with little care in the world, not an ounce of shame in his game. I put together later, this was another time he drugged me (with my own stuff) and had others over to assault me once I was asleep.

That night as people came over, he grabbed their fee's as they walked through the door. Sitting my unconscious body on the bed and inserting things into me, laughing. While taking videos and pictures. I won't go into more details than that, but you can start to see the pattern.

My common sense thinks they were part of a larger network of likeminded individuals, using the dark web to connect. Sending seemingly harmless messages from one computer to the next, letting each other know when someone had access to an unsuspecting victim. Money was exchanged, and lives were ruined with a click of a button. A game more extensive than me, but I was an easy target, helpless, sickly, and naive.

The fact is that when I was on drugs, they were the only thing that mattered. The suspicious behavior I saw wasn't worth my time, or so I thought. When I look back sometimes it's hard to have that compassion, I was talking about. The truth is, not only did I not think Damien would do something like this....I didn't even give him the credit that he could. Our conversations were minimal and let's just say he put on the jar head mask to seem less intelligent (at least we know where he got that from). He played chess with my life, and I was convinced I could beat him at checkers. His big D energy walked all over my glass heart.

You've got to keep in mind that I'm writing this in hindsight, after watching the entire reenactment. I couldn't believe it when all this came to the surface. Never in a million years would I imagine my family doing such things, or him playing me for a fool for profit.

I suspect this is around the same time he met Jera, but it wasn't me who introduced them. I knew her, and to put two of my closest enemies together would've been suicide. At least that's how I saw it.

He dropped me off at the treatment center acting sweet and loving, because he knew I'd be around people who'd tell me to get rid of him. I wanted him gone at that point with every cell in my body, but he had a guilt trip on me that was hard to shake.

Manipulated Memories

This next section is my reencounter with Jordan, but since neither of us remembered each other, I'll retell it as though we were meeting for the first time. To keep you able to see how it went down from my perspective. When I heard he lived in the same town as my dad, and his cousin was one of my best friends in elementary school, it seemed weird that we'd never met.

I was brought into the building on a stretcher, too weak to walk from withdrawal. Our eyes met as they rolled me into my room, and I was initially repulsed by his long beard. But, even then, he was the most handsome man I'd ever seen. There was something about him that caught my attention in a way I'd never known. Almost like a karmic lesson had been activated. That no matter how hard I tried, wouldn't let go of me until it was done. A voice in my head said he was in my life to teach me about my insecurities. I ignored that hint with my rose-colored glasses snug on my face.

My energy field craved him, after that first encounter. Jordan was now a grown man in great shape. Three and a half years younger with the attitude of an 18-year-old. Still, I was smitten and determined to make him mine. Within a few days, I found the courage to ask him to sit and talk with me outside. He looked at me with surprise, like, why me? We talked for hours that day, and it felt like chatting to an old friend. We both sensed that I could read his thoughts, which was interesting to experience with someone I barely knew. There was something between us that I'd never faced, and it was helpless to resist. He seemed just as interested by asking questions about who I was and why I was there. I told him about Damien and my desire to escape.

Jordan was the epitome of Sagittarius energy, jovial and outgoing, something I desperately wanted to be. He couldn't help but dance when a song he liked came on, and flirt with every person he talked to, no matter age or gender. Charisma poured off him in buckets, leaving males and females entranced in his unbounding confidence. He had just as many haters as I did, and it was nice that someone could relate.

We'd sneak around the treatment center touching hands as we walked past. Meeting in our special spot on the side of the building, hidden by trees. Taking turns playing music, slowly inching closer and closer to one another like magnets. Rebelling against the non-fraternizing rules by sitting in the public areas using a sweatshirt to hide our holding hands, giggling like school kids. I'd stare at him for minutes at a time, and he'd pride-fully act like he didn't notice. His features seemed perfectly sculpted out of clay. My ideal looking partner in every way, and he was dangerously aware of it.

To have some privacy, we walked around town on our off time. Slowly strolling through parks and sitting on benches to enjoy each other's company. If I'd thought about Damien for even a moment, I would've been more careful. I knew he'd stalked me in SD, so why would he just stop doing that now. Spoiler alert, he didn't, and at some point, he saw us together. This was a betrayal in his eyes that wouldn't go without punishment.

Manipulated Memories

I haven't spoken much about Damiens idiosyncrasies because I dislike telling people's secrets, but there were certain things that made this worse than others. He didn't appreciate the culture he'd come from the same way others do. He'd speak about my white privilege and his bitterness towards the world because of his darker skin. So, for me to be dating a blonde hair, blue eyed man was like throwing gasoline on an already out of control wildfire.

I was too caught up with the falling in love thing to even think twice about what I was doing. My crippling naivety thought that Jordan and I'd be together forever, and he'd protect me. Another scenario that makes me laugh out loud. Pure comedy, you'll see. I didn't know it, but Damien must've not left my hometown right away, because him and Jera began an affair behind the scenes. Using their hatred for me as conversation fuel.

It was forbidden to have relationships while in recovery, but everyone knew what was happening with me and Jordan. After he broke up with (or said he did) the girl he was seeing at the time, we gradually became a couple. Within a month, we were inseparable. Any chance to look at him was worth leaving class, and I found myself straying from my program. The intensity of our partnership grew until I didn't know what to do with it. Every kiss was so electrifying the sexual tension became unbearable. When he shaved his beard, that was it, I knew I was ready to take it to the next level, and I happily gave in to his temptation.

This rehab happened to be in a hospital building that didn't have an emergency room. So, at night, everything closed, and luckily for us there were only a couple of security guards patrolling the area. Making it easy to sneak around and have sex on the bench tables or inside the smoking tents. Nervous and paranoid but excited. Anywhere and anytime we could, it was fun and freeing to be so reckless. Once I even snuck in his room and made his roommate leave while we fooled around.

But I felt him pulling away a couple weeks before his discharge date. Not knowing what to do, I became obsessive and irritating. We'd text back and forth, and I'd never be satisfied with his answers. Constantly probing annoying questions and making insinuations. I can see now that I pushed him away from the fear of losing him. I knew it was over the day he told me he loved me. It looked painful for him to say, almost like he didn't mean to, it just came out. Whether he meant it or not, his ego wanted to be free.

The day he left was hard for me when he couldn't even bring himself to kiss me one last time. He thought it was best that I let him go, because he was going straight back to drugs. And once again, another guy left me for my own good, (at least that's what they tell themselves). I cried for weeks. Devastated beyond repair for a long time. I choked on my heartbreak when someone asked me about him and struggled to keep up with my treatment goals.

It turned out that after Damien saw us together, he used lies to get to Jordan after he left the program. Claiming I was a gross slut that deserved to be messed with, introducing him to Jera at a bar. My gifts showed me their interactions, but time doesn't exist in the quantum field. In order for me to give you specific dates and times, there'd need to be some serious detective work done.

For Jera those two were toys. Drug buddies and sex partners at best, nothing more. People she could gossip with about me, a favorite pass time now that she'd been programmed to hate me. Because she had standards they didn't meet, no matter how cute they were. She had a life set up that she didn't plan to ruin, but she was always down for a side piece and hurting me was a bonus. Her desire to win at all costs meant anyone I was involved with was fair game. The three of them began a trio of darkness, which was exactly what the projects had been hoping for.

I relapsed right after Jordan left, but the center let me finish anyway. Everyone around me said I told you so and noted that they tried to warn me. Like I was predetermined to suffer just for knowing him, and they were right.

To my surprise, a month later, he called me, the morning after a miserably failed date with someone else. As my phone rang, I snuck into the hotel bathroom to talk. He asked me where I was, and I made up a lie. He demanded I take an Uber he sent for me to his friend's house. I was so excited that I grabbed my things and made an excuse to my date that I had to leave. A slutty move, but I didn't care. I left my personal belongings in the room and said I'd be back for them later.

Manipulated Memories

I showed up so excited I couldn't stop smiling, and he introduced me to his friends, as they sat drinking and watching football. Right away, he pulled me into a separate room wanting sex. I mean, I knew that was coming, but I hadn't showered yet. So, I decided to make it sexy instead of embarrassing by asking him to shower with me. Which when I think about it now, kinda says I had my own charisma, thank you very much. We danced in the water like we had done it a thousand times and had sex in the connected room although he was emotionally distant. I noticed something off about the way he smelled, and I mentioned it. He apologized but barely looked at me. The drugs he was on, had ruined his once sultry pheromones and turned them into a toxic odor. He kept sniveling and tipping his head to release the cocaine. I felt bad for him, sad that he couldn't be as happy as I was or feel the overflowing love that drained out of me and into his undeserving hands.

The night went smoothly except for the hour he spent in the bathroom alone, doing more drugs. I let him be and sat in silence waiting. When he was done, we sat on the roof holding each other, and he told romantic lies to appease the moment. Then ghosted me like it never happened, and I was devastated again, although this time I was pissed I'd walked into the trap.

Chapter 15

Knowing your own darkness is the best method for dealing with the darkness of other people.
~ Carl Jung

I threw myself into making art, to be distracted from my misery. After I found androgenous masquerade masks at Michaels and had a spark of inspiration to decorate them. I played around with unusual color patterns and jewels, and the ideas flew out of me in beautiful designs. Each one representing an aspect of myself or the battles I'd been through. And as a collection they express how humans are all Source consciousness with different faces. They came out in ways I couldn't have planned, and I loved the freedom I found in the process. I could be anything I wanted to be on the canvas.

Mid November, Dominic of all people called and came to lunch with me, on one of my days off. He seemed proud and yet sad in a way I couldn't put my finger on. We had a good time, and I did well keeping my hands to myself, although I didn't want to. I could tell that even after fifteen years, I was still as in love with him as ever. No matter who I'd loved in between. And yet it was a simple meeting with no insinuation of anything else that kept him in the back of my mind for years.

Somehow I got back in contact with Jaylan, and left treatment. We spent a few days together and I learned he was about to have a baby, so that was that. I decided rather quickly I wanted to use again, and the cycle of regrets repeated. My drive for drugs was wholly irrational, and I couldn't even control the amount I took anymore. After trading a tablet for a few grams of speed I was off to the races. Sitting in my bathroom for hours in the middle of the night while my mother slept in my room. She woke up the next morning to find me hiding in the closet after all of it was gone in twelve hours. I couldn't explain to her that I couldn't move. Trying my hardest but unable to pass the invisible barrier that separated me from the world.

Something strange began to happen inside me. I looked down at my hands, stunned, but not sure why. Then a separate part of myself jumped into my mind. I could feel her hiding, holding onto me for dear life. It was the other soul who'd been with me all these years, she was scared. I thought I was losing it, because I could sense she didn't want to be here anymore, and this was her way of keeping safe. I knew she wasn't me, and it was terrifying. I couldn't tell anyone because I didn't understand it myself, until I learned about the walk-in contract so many years later.

My mother eventually left, and I was back on the drug scene alone, but now I kept seeing repeating numbers everywhere. It started with 1111 every few days on my phone and clocks. I couldn't have known how big of a life changing experience this would be.

At the same time, I was drowning in a world of deep sadness, and the only thing I knew to do about it was run back to Damien. With three months left on my lease, I irresponsibly left my apartment and traveled to Florida. Where he'd moved, while I was in treatment. Giving in to my painfully complex trauma bonded codependency. Convinced that we were two people so broken no one else could understand us.

The awakening seemed to intensify my emotions, and after getting to his house and analyzing the situation, I knew I didn't deserve what he was doing anymore. I stopped talking altogether, which angered him even more, because he lived for my reactions. Sadistically getting off on the pain and suffering his torment caused me. No matter what I did, he became rageful. I stayed only because he made me feel worthless and told me no one would ever love me differently.

One morning I woke up foggy with an abscess on the back of my leg. Damien had a fit when he had to take me to the hospital to get it lanced open. A vision showed me he and his friends had let a scorpion dance on my skin in the middle of the night. It's sting causing the puss filled wound.

Manipulated Memories

To block out the abuse, I began to meditate. Finally listening to the many different treatment center's advice. Which helped me scrounge up enough courage to leave. With the help of a friend, I took a three-day Greyhound bus back to San Diego. Noticing right away that security was on me in full force. More people made themselves known by driving past, and yelling profanities. This time it was scarier because I was on my own. I only lasted two weeks before I was back in Florida with Damien. I kept thinking he was my saving grace from the intimidation. I kept buying into the lies about how he'd changed and promised he wouldn't hurt me this time. It was a game, a power play that grew his ego.

He picked me up from the airport giddy, smiling from ear to ear. His happiness soothed me, but I knew it wouldn't last. We stopped at the grocery store, and he bought me whatever food I wanted, an improvement that wouldn't endure. He took my bags up the two flights of stairs, and once again I was a prisoner. To remove the dirtiness I felt, I jumped in the bath immediately, and to my surprise, he jumped in with me. Professing his love while washing my hair. He seemed genuinely sad for me for once. I slept the entire rest of the day, waking at four a.m. to an empty bed. As I walked into the living room, he suspiciously shut his computer. "What are you doing?" I asked. "Nothing."

He walked towards me with a big smile, bending down and picking me up, wrapping my legs around his waist, saying, "I love you; I'm so glad you're here, don't ever leave me again, please," caressing me with the softest touch, and we headed to the bedroom. He pleased me sexually, which was a welcome change, one he knew was necessary to keep me there this time. Using his sexual power to distract me from questioning what he was doing awake.

After a couple of days, he had a complete crisis meltdown again. His soul forcing out of him the details of some of his worst mistakes. It was painful to watch as his darkest truths were pushed beyond his ability to hold the guilt. Recalling in detail his atrocities about sleeping with a thirteen-year-old when he was twenty-two, and how her family found out and almost killed him. It hurt my heart for that poor girl, and I had difficulty looking at him. I could feel there was more to it that he wasn't telling me. I watched in shock as he emotionally vomited stories about his tragic experiences in Iraq. While crying and screaming, he forced me to listen to the sadistic twisted occurrences that shouldn't have happened. I sat motionless, unable to speak, with my head down. Silently praying he didn't take it out on me. The pressure must've been eating him alive, and it was clear he had to tell someone. Like a part of him wanted to get caught for the unnecessary savagery. To hear how disturbed he truly was scared me.

That incident put me in a predicament. What was I supposed to do about this information? On the one hand, the young girl's family knew what happened, and the decision not to press charges was on them, not me. But the things that he recalled about his deployment…were so far out of the realm of acceptable, even for a war zone, that it terrified me.

Manipulated Memories

Out of nowhere he handed me a brand-new tablet and said, "I got this for you." "What for?" I rightfully questioned his motives. "I wanted to do something nice for you." In my head I knew something was fishy, but I took it. Looking back at this now I know he used it to track me, and I should've put that together because he never bought me anything, ever.

The fighting got worse and worse until I managed to scrounge up enough money to leave, and once again make my way back to San Diego.

After spending a couple of nights at a veteran homeless shelter being harassed, I managed to get my cousin to let me stay with her since we'd been close when I was little. I left my clothes in her garage and slept on the couch. Helping with her kids as much as I could, and I loved spending time with them, but within a couple weeks I couldn't stop my cravings any longer.

I met up with another veteran from treatment; we'll call him Johny. Someone I'd stayed in contact with over the years and genuinely believed was a dear friend. Who was doing the same things I was, and I should've known better. We got high at the downtown library, and I couldn't help but tell him what Damien had said about the underaged girl. I was freaked out and needed someone else to know. I'd find out he was the worst person I could've told.

I managed to make it back to Erin's house when I couldn't stay with my cousin any longer. Finding myself again physically sick and unable to take care of myself. And once again, I hesitantly called Damien begging for a plane ticket to his house. His reaction was one of concern and support, "Of course, I'm so happy you're coming home," cruelly, lying through his teeth. "I've got you a flight for six o'clock, but you have a layover in Houston." For a moment, I was relieved I wouldn't have to struggle for a place to stay or worry about being followed. We chatted for a few minutes about how excited he was to have sex with me, and I already regretted that he was my only option, but I wanted to feel safe. I knew the bullying from the stalkers would stop if he was around, and I couldn't take one more second of it. You'd think by now I'd put together his part in all of it, but I was blinded by love.

After packing my things, I headed to the airport, where Erin dropped me off with some words of concern. As he pulled away, I heard a voice I thought I recognized in the distance. I spun on my heels to see who it was, but no one was there. Anxiety rose from deep within my chest as I checked my bags, knowing I had to act normal. I shrugged it off, "It's probably nothing," continuing to the counter. Snickering behind me stopped me in my tracks when it sounded an awful lot like Damien and Jordan. My brain automatically said that wasn't possible, "They don't even know each other." I shook my head and told myself, "It's just the drugs talking." I got my ticket and headed to the bathroom to do the last of my stash before I had to throw it out.

While sitting in the silence of the restroom, BANG, BANG, someone smashed their fist on the door. My heart jumped out of my chest, and my muscles froze. I slowly opened it, but no one was there. Instead, the noise of laughter surrounded me. Imprisoned by my paranoia, my ears perked up, scanning the sounds, picking out three distinctive voices. Damien, Jordan, and Johny. Was it possible they were a part of what'd been happening recently? I couldn't say, nor could I handle the possibility. Then an unrecognizable female voice loudly giggled and made harsh comments about what a wreck I was.

Trying to soothe the fear, I looked in the mirror and gave myself a pep talk, "No one is here, you haven't slept in a while, you're just tired." I dumped my paraphernalia and headed towards the plane. On route, the voices threw out mean jabs and comments, while poking at my insecurities. I swore I saw Jordan out of the corner of my eye, and turned in a circle trying to find him, but he was gone. Then Damien's undeniable evil laugh sounded from the other side of the room.

My mind searched desperately for answers. Why would Damien and Jordan be following me in an airport? What would be the point? I maneuvered behind a soda machine to see the people walking by nearly hysterical. The same voices found their way to me from the only direction I couldn't see. My heart pounded, and my ego shattered, tears poured down my face as I searched for why. "I must be hallucinating; they don't even know each other." I found out the answer's years later, but I was so in love with Jordan that my heart couldn't accept this reality. That these boys made it their business to torture me, after I'd told Damien's deepest secrets.

Manipulated Memories

They full force went along with the ideas and thoughts planted into their minds out of pride. Even enjoying the game of cat and mouse, because they felt strong and powerful, to watch as I hugged my knees and cried, listening to their ridicule and belittlement. Eventually, I pulled it together the best I could and made my way to the security check. I'd been in the same clothes for days and became painfully embarrassed to take off my smelly shoes while walking through the machine. My mind told me it was an appropriate sentence to my lack of cleanliness, so I kept my head low and stared at the carpet. The cackling seemed to rattle from all directions now, and I could feel their fingers pointing. I was mortified when they began to chuckle about how thin and sickly I was. Meth always gave me a frail skinniness I couldn't escape, and I hated what I had become.

My head kept reassuring me they weren't there, but again, I saw Jordan from my peripheral, and my heart sank. Could this really be happening? I got my things from the conveyer belt and went to my gate, waiting there for the plane too scared to move. Spending the entire time searching the crowd for the outlines of the people I knew so well. I thought I saw them a couple times but couldn't be sure. I put my headphones on and ignored the world till it was time to go.

It was possible that they boarded last with first-class tickets. That would mean I wouldn't see them getting on or off the plane. And if it was true, it was a brilliant plan that took some guts to pull off, but I couldn't trust what I was hearing or seeing at that point. The flight was uneventful, besides my brain running in circles trying to put together a scenario that made sense. When we got to Houston, it all began again. My drugs kicked in, and the racing thoughts turned into a hurricane of anxiety and apprehension. I was in a full-blown panic walking through baggage claim and outside to smoke a cigarette, where the ridicule began again. "You're a slut!" from one direction. "We never loved you," from another. My world tore apart. "You're a joke, you always have been!" bounced off the cement pillars, over and over, crippling my soul.

My hands shaking so badly I could barely hold the cigarette straight. I tried keeping myself calm by noting that it was highly improbable Damien and Jordan even knew each other, and Johny hated Damien. Nothing about any of it made logical sense. It felt like the most surreal experience that could ever happen, and I tried to keep it together, but there was no hope for that. I'm sure I looked like a lunatic stalking the crowd for answers. Quietly crying uncontrollably, barely able to form sentences.

After the short layover, I'd been enduring this for hours. The fear wore on my face, and my bloodshot eyes burned. Walking up the escalator towards my gate, a police officer asked me if I was okay, and a tidal wave of emotion flew out of my mouth. I wanted to scream and run but I had no energy left. I couldn't hold inside what was happening, and I blurted out the situation.

Which sounded like a prescription for a straitjacket. He looked around, decided it wasn't possible and gently escorted me into his police cruiser claiming he wanted to help. But instead drove me downtown to a mental health facility. To most people, my life would seem inconceivable. He dropped me off at the most bizarre crazy house I'd ever seen (and I've seen plenty). I walked in, and they talked to me in whispers, "Are you okay?" Like anyone who was okay would be there. "No," I matched their tone, and described what happened. They told me everything was going to be fine. I should try and relax because I was safe. They lulled me out of my truth and into their delusion of rationality (something this world has a hard-on for). I got out of my clothes and into a cheap light blue well-used robe. They gave me something for the anxiety, but I was past pharmaceutical help.

Emotionally I was despondent, angry and confused, because I wanted answers. "Sneaky bastards got me again. Just another day of me playing looking like an idiot. That was it, my life is officially a joke." I neurotically took the blame for their wild behavior. Still unable to see that the more I thought of my life as a joke. The more it became one.

Inside the hospital looked like the beginning of a psychological thriller, dark low-lighting and stale white walls. They walked me into a locked room with twenty brown, plush reclining chairs, and nothing else. I sat in one, and they let me know I could request anything I needed. "You need to rest," they prescribed. I had no choice but to sit with my unbelievable story.

For three days, I lounged, ate, and thought about things. While doctors persuaded me, I made it all up. "Drugs make us think crazy things," they said, and I believed them. Which is sad because I could've gotten away from them at that point. If doctors for once would have trusted me. I could've had less pain and suffering if I'd just trusted myself. Instead, I listened to their lies and called Damien. He acted like he was heartbroken I hadn't shown up and bought me another flight back to him.

My flight had an overnight stop in a random city in between us, so I called an uber to take me to a hotel. I was sick again from withdrawal and didn't want to go to Damien's without some cash. So when the driver asked me for sex, I reluctantly said "100$." He agreed and I serviced him without saying a word, holding back the vomit in my throat.

Chapter 16

Drugs take you to hell, disguised as heaven.
~ Donald Frost

Once again, Damien and I began fighting as soon as I got there. I didn't understand that now he knew I told Johny what he did, and our relationship was coming to a head. After a relaxing day and making a well-balanced dinner of chicken and vegetables, his favorite. We were right back to where we started, after he decided we'd been happy long enough. "Do you love Jordan?" he asked. "No," I fibbed. "Yes, you do!" he pouted. I buckled in for a long night and sank into the couch. "No, Damien, I only love you," I lied. "You hate me, don't you?" We were both quiet for a moment, and I saw the storm brewing in his eyes. Chest raised, he got up from his armchair and shuffled in my direction, to stand over me on the couch. "Is he prettier than me?" Evil sparkled in his glossy eyes. "No, of course not," I tried to appease his vanity.

Jealous passion flashed over his face as he grabbed my left ankle with one hand and jerked me onto the ground, pulling me like a caveman across the apartment. I stayed quiet and let it happen. He lifted me up by the armpits and threw me onto the dining room sofa. Then grabbed a stool and drug it to sit directly in front of me, he grabbed my face hard with both hands, and shouted louder and louder, "You're a slut, a stupid whore." With no shame that the entire complex could hear his verbal violence. "Yes, Damien, I'm sorry," I pleaded. "Do you want to fuck him? He asked without looking for a response. "No, Damien, I'm here with you," I responded softly. "He's hot, I saw a picture of him. You still love him and want to fuck him, don't you," He accused. "No, Damien, I don't," I said in a hushed tone. "I do," he replied, grinning from ear to ear.

Something was strange about that statement, I mean he was always wild, but this was primal. Like a shield that kept him human had broken. Like an animal who just escaped his cage was deciding its next move. That last sentence should've been my first clue, but I figured he was just trying to scare me. But really, he was trying to hold himself back from what he actually wanted to do, rip me apart limb from limb.

His feelings grew and grew as he held my face yelling profanities. Defeated, I said nothing, convinced I deserved it because I was such a mess. Trapped sitting opposite him for hours, listening to his pent-up rage spew all over me. When he went into the bathroom after a couple hours, I ran and jumped in bed, throwing the blankets over my head. He stomped in when he was done and ripped the covers from me, turned on the light and stood with arms crossed as I curled into a ball. He slapped my legs and told me to get up. It was after three in the morning, and I was exhausted. I begged him to let me sleep, and he said no with a smirk. Pushing me back to the dining room sofa, continuing his verbal assaults that sounded more like gibberish and erratic nonsense.

He stood up and walked into the kitchen and for a second, I felt relieved he might leave me alone for a minute. Until I saw him stare at the knife block and in slow motion pull the biggest one out. "Wait, Damien, you'd regret killing me, and you know it," He brought the butcher knife back with him to the stool, sat down and set it on his lap, still crying and confused. "I love you, Morgan, and I hate you." "I know, it's okay."

I finally found the courage to push the voice record app on my phone. Knowing I may need it as evidence one day, whether I was alive or not. Fumbling his words, he leaned forward with the knife, and I put my hands over my face. He slid the blade into and up the right sleeve of my sweatshirt, slowly slicing the fabric like butter. I sunk back and gave him the space to cut when I realized what he was doing. Destroying it because it was my favorite.

"I'm scared I might kill you." Was the last sentence I heard before a long pause as he lit a cigarette. I've just now (many years later) figured out that he'd been wrestling with his internal commands to kill me for years. The projects didn't just intend to harm us. They wanted us to end each other. If he killed me then he'd go to prison and that'd be two down in one shot.

In a calm voice I suggested another option, "Okay, then can I call your family?" I knew someone could talk him out of it if they knew what was going on. It was early morning now and eventually he let me call his mom. I told her what happened, and she came over within minutes. I showed her the recording of his screaming but left out everything else, and she looked shocked. I don't think she'd ever seen him act that way. She spoke to him like a child and acted like it wasn't a big deal.

After packing my stuff, she brought me to the train station and bought a bus ticket back to San Diego. On the ride home, I thought about his control issues, and desires to have sex with the same people I did, ignoring the comment he'd made about Jordan. I thought that in his mind he wanted him, just to say he did. His obsession was so strong that if I'd slept with someone, he wanted them to. That might not sound like it makes sense, but the project leaders messed with his desire for me sexually. Saying that I was made for him and no one else.

The journey to SD this time was intense, and I missed two buses on the way. When I got back to the west coast, I realized none of my belongings came with. Someone from the bus had stolen everything, leaving me stranded in Cali with nothing.

My heart and mind craved to escape and yet doing drugs just made me feel worse. I needed treatment. My only places to stay were with people still using, which felt overwhelming. The voices, the lack of stability, and the inner calling to be a better person had all created a spiral of negativity. I stayed high all day and cried all night.

Spending time with Erin wasn't what it used to be. When we met at VVSD, we weren't close; he was at least ten years older and a regular churchgoer. Not my cup of tea. After a couple of years, we both returned, and he was one of the few people I knew, so we started talking. Our personalities seemed to match, and I thought he was a genuinely lovely person. Hard to find in the aggressive mix of type A's at the center.

Most ex-military members (me included) have a chip on their shoulder towards the rest of the world, but Erin had a sweet disposition. Everyone looked at me funny for getting close to him, but we'd become the best of friends for years. He helped me whenever I needed him, no matter what, and I forced him to have fun whenever I could.

He would fix my car, and I'd make him bike with me on the beach. I trusted him with my life, knowing good and well no one was safe. We were both heavy-duty drug users but never judged each other. Since he only did meth, I didn't have to worry he'd be sick. And I could count on him to help me get well if that's what it came to. We had very few other friends for the first few years. Then he got a girlfriend, and something changed, he constantly complained to me about her, and I'm sure vice versa.

After spending time with his girlfriend, who graciously gave me some new clothes, I felt better enough to walk around town and look for old associates to find more drugs. I scrolled through my phone looking for someone to meet, when out of the blue, I was pulled off the concrete and forced into a car that took me to an unknown location. Within minutes I was drugged and unconscious. Someone laid my body on a bed lined with clear crinkled plastic, and five men and one woman entered the room. The group began dancing and gyrating like they were go-go dancers at a sleezy club, laughing and repeating Latin incantations into a high crescendo. Creating a dark pagan ritual on a random weekday.

The thing about dark magic is that it's always temporary, and there's no way to get out of the accruing karma. So, whether or not these people in the short term got what they wanted, the universal laws would catch up with them eventually. To empower the spell, they began to have sex with each other and me simultaneously. Each one pulling out different weapons and sodomizing me one at a time. While the others poured random food and powders onto my skin as they jumped around like wild hyenas.

The group kept injecting me with a sedative to keep me asleep but accidentally overdosed me. Everyone in the crew panicked, and one of them insisted they take me to the hospital. While nearly hysterical and running into each other yelling curse words, two of them scrambled me into the backseat of a vehicle. Everyone was talking over each other and flailing about, unsure if I'd die or not. Shouting at each other and highlighting their stupidity. Every one of them lighting up a cigarette and making plans to flee the country, as they drove to the nearest hospital. When they pulled into the complex, one guy jumped out and ran to the front to retrieve a wheelchair, as the others pulled me from the car. Their bloodshot eyes as wide as saucers, barely able to blink. They rolled me into the ER department sliding me into the center of the hospital. Then let go of the handles, turned and ran as fast as they could outside.

During this debacle, the other soul I'd started this life with, decided she'd had enough, and left the body as I laid on the gurney. Just like the brain had to be completely unconscious to let me in, it had to be again to allow her to leave. So this entire fiasco was a blessing in disguise.

From above my body, I heard yelling and saw people scrambling, then felt something weird in my chest, so I held my sternum. People in scrubs rushed around my bedside messing with monitors and fluids. I had flat lined. They saved me with a shot of adrenaline/Narcan straight into the heart and I woke up vomiting with a plastic bag held to my mouth. The room was foggy and buzzing with life. My hearing took the longest of my senses to return. Even when it did, I wasn't able to focus. I stared at the nurses as they glared at me with disapproval. Looking down, I saw puncture wounds on my arms and hands that weren't there before. Confused and delusional, I tried to put the story together.

After only a few minutes the hospital workers told me to get up and get out, in a rude tone. I was trying to figure out what happened, and I knew they believed it was my fault, but I wasn't awake enough to argue. At that point the only way to make sense of things was to blame myself anyway, I could control that. I couldn't handle the level of pressure it'd mean if I thought about how much danger I was really in. I stood up by holding the railing of the bed, and one excruciating step after another, made my way out the room. After pulling the curtains back I noticed a man sitting in a chair just outside my door. A 5'2 dark complexion Spanish man had been waiting for me. He got up and walked beside me smiling, as I went towards the exit. He met my gait and slid next to me and said, "You can come to my house." I was so out of it from dying that I did what he said.

We walked back to his house/tiny room with stained floors that smelled like dirt. Only stopping our miles long trip on foot, to get a couple beers from a gas station. The bed at his place was barely big enough for one, and the only other items in his room were a dresser and a chair. It was cleverly hidden behind an apartment building where no one could see or hear. I laid down alone after drinking the alcohol and fell asleep quickly. Waking up in the middle of the night being raped again. Unable to say no or move, I just let it happen. I'd been through it so many times by then, that it didn't even phase me anymore, I was completely numb. "My punishment for going home with a stranger," I thought. I was too weak from the medication to try and put up a fight anyway.

In the morning, he walked me to a convenience store, and when I looked around at the location we were in, I noticed it was the same area Damien's "cousin" lived. A place I'd visited more than once. The slimy man bought me a candy bar name Carlos, a reference to an argument Damien and I'd had just a few days prior. There was no more guessing, this was retaliation. Whether Damien was a part of it or not, I couldn't know. Before he left, I asked him for five bucks for a bus ticket, and he said, "You're not worth it."

I put my head down and walked towards Erin's house. Looking through my purse to see what if anything was in it. No credit cards, money or drugs but my phone although dead, was still there. My ego was crushed by his words, and there was no hope left. I didn't know it, but three different groups were after me now. The projects, the Mexican traffickers (possibly cartel) and Damien's friends. At that moment, I couldn't find the connection between each event. The best I could do was go home and try to hide.

The entire idea of who I was felt wrong now. Like shrinking into oblivion was going to be the only way to survive. My young unearned confidence was gone, and drugs couldn't fake it for me anymore. I barely spoke and if I did, I didn't trust what I was saying. Reality didn't make sense, so I didn't feel entitled to an opinion. My life continued to prove to me what I'd been taught as a child. That I couldn't trust myself.

I decided to stay at the homeless shelter again because I felt bad for making Erin take care of me. After a few days, my clothes started going missing, and I knew intuitively even then, that someone was paying someone to mess with me. The constant fear and methamphetamines kept me unable to sleep in the giant tent filled with homeless addicts. Something told me to get out as fast as I could, so I begged my mom to buy me a train ticket home, and she luckily agreed. I reluctantly called Erin to help me get to the station the next day, and he let me come over and stay the night. Beyond grateful, I threw what I had left in his car.

When we got to his girlfriend's house to visit, I noticed that some jerk put a pair of men's boxers smeared with dog feces in my backpack when I wasn't looking. Ashamed by it, I snuck 'em out and left it on the floor without telling anyone. I'd find out later that Erin's girlfriend thought they were his, and I'd just pissed off my only friend.

We left early to catch the train in the morning, but because of traffic, we pulled into the parking lot seconds too late. I watched it roar past me while I shuffled my stuff on the platform. The station personnel said I could catch the next one, but I had a few hours to kill so I walked to a park nearby to get high.

Once I got to the clearing behind the mall, I introduced myself to a group of people, looking to be friendly and network. And didn't hesitate to start a conversation, although I knew better. I wanted to believe that the world was a safe place. I wanted it so much that I would continue to act like it was. I never let the truth of my situation turn me against others. Although maybe at that time it should have. I was recklessly oblivious to my surroundings because I couldn't allow myself to believe what was actually going on. I know I keep saying that, but I feel a need to reiterate the understanding that I couldn't handle my predicament, so I acted like it didn't happen. This behavior is appalling to me now, I would never let this kind of thing happen again. And yet as I write this story, I get it. When there is such intense danger in your life, it cancels each other out. How was I supposed to act? Bitter, angry, hostile? Was I supposed to scream and yell at the cops who didn't believe me? Or my family who didn't care? Was it Erin's problem to solve? Was it the worlds? Or was it mine, and mine alone? Was I capable of doing anything about it? No. So this is what I did. I smiled and giggled and complimented people. I forced myself to create a world that didn't exist. A safe, loving, fun world. Where I could talk to random strangers and be totally fine.

A large hand grabbed me around the mouth from behind, as I put a shot of dope together. I was dragged and pulled into an already packed car and shoved onto the floorboards. I woke up miles away with my butt in the air and face in the dirt. My knees piercing the gravel and cement beneath, with more mysterious puncture wounds on my arms and deep gashes on my elbows and knees. As the mental fog lifted, I stood up and scanned the environment. Something was off, but I didn't know what. Looking down at my feet jarred me. Was I wearing different shoes? I slowly shifted my gaze up my body and noticed I was in a completely different outfit altogether. I put my hand in my waistband and pulled the front of them out, to look down. "Oh, my God, they shaved me." I noticed from the sensation that my armpits were bare as well.

My head kept ringing, and the trauma compounded once I saw that all my important things were missing. No phone, but no one to call that could provide any safety anyway. No drugs or cigarettes left to ease the suffering and no one to blame but myself. Looking around, I didn't recognize the location. There were abandoned houses to my left and a homeless man sitting on a step playing with a phone. I walked up to him asking if it was mine. He said no but I was suspicious anyway. Didn't matter, I wasn't fighting him for it. In the distance, I saw a cop stopped a block away and ran to him, blurting out what just happened. Telling him, I was raped and left for dead. He looked at me like I was crazy and walked away without saying a word.

I had no choice but to go back to Erin's, with nothing to my name. As I walked to his house in complete despair with my head down, and tears streaming across my face, I tried to put things together. How was all this happening to me? How could one person go through so much heartbreak? Defeated, alone, and confused, I was undecided if I would tell him. He wouldn't believe me anyway, of course. Why would he? My life looked more like a movie every day. For him, it was exhausting, and I didn't want to be a burden. The intensity of my life was too much for anyone, I understood that, it was for me too. After arriving and sitting on his doorstep for hours waiting, he showed up without sympathy. It was late, and I was inconsolable, barely able to speak anyway.

I called my mom in a panic and begged for another train ticket home. I couldn't believe it when she said yes without confrontation. I was finally getting the fuck out of Cali for good. Erin went to the store and grabbed a couple of beers to help me relax. After what I just went through, drugs would never be the same, and I wasn't interested in that. When I went to the bathroom, he must have spiked my drink.

Let me clue you in on a secret if you don't know anything about drugs. Quite frequently, men who do meth are sexual predators. And Erin had a XXX film setup in his bedroom. I knew it was there but never worried about that. He'd always been good to me. We were close, really close. And I thought he cared for me as deeply as I cared for him. But money is hard to pass up when you're a drug addict. So the boys club paid Erin to use that equipment. I would never have thought it possible, but like I said, his soul was replaced long ago.

After another night of being videotaped in the worst way, I woke up with my privates throbbing, looking around, and Erin was nowhere to be seen. My heart was tattered and my nervous system in shock. Noticing right away that the door to the apartment was wide open. A detail that told the entire story. The horrific game I found myself in had just destroyed my last relationship. My best friend was now one of them, maybe he always was. Maybe that's why he was the only person I was allowed to stay with to Damian. I was in a surreal world of lies, drug mobsters, idiot boys and violence. Out of my league when it came to the people I was dealing with and helplessly alone.

I looked through the stuff I had left there and found the tablet Damien gave me. Thinking I could sell it for a phone, I took it with me.

Manipulated Memories

I begged a drug associate/friend to give me a ride back to the train station.

Chapter 17

Make it through the night, there's a brighter day.
~Tupac Shakur

I returned to the San Diego Old Town Amtrak station, on May 1st, 2018; mentally, physically, and emotionally exhausted, stumbling my way onto the northbound train heading towards Washington State. While taking my seat, I prayed under my breath, "Source, please help me make it home." My mind was barely functioning and regretfully clouded by chemicals. My body painfully fragile, every bone ached, and my cells screamed for nourishment. I hadn't eaten in days, and I struggled to stand up straight from the fatigue.

Nothing about the events leading up to this made sense, and my thought processing was overloaded from battling my own mind. Overwhelming hopelessness enveloped my will to live, suffocating it. At the same time, my heart was drowning in the tragedy of it all. Was it possible it would all disappear if I ignored it? Could I live happily, disregarding the sexual exploitation and traumatic events of my life? I doubted it but tried anyway. Confused, smelly, tired, hungry, and penniless, I took my seat, head low. Dreading the long trip ahead, searching for answers I knew wouldn't come. Without my memories, I couldn't help but obsessively search for answers to the questions that eluded me. What were these puncture holes all over my body? How did I get these deep scratches and scrapes on my feet and elbows? Who was it that took me to his house from the hospital, and how did the staff allow that to happen? As far as waking up across town with my face in the dirt, my brain ignored that completely. And the fact that Erin had allowed people into his house was too much for me. I was barely able to keep one foot in front of the other, let alone accept anything more than what I'd already remembered.

These questions were so outrageous that denying them was the only way to keep from losing my mind. What I was aware of was already enough to test the foundation of who I was.

While swimming in deep contemplation, my intuition perked up warning me of possible danger. Which would've been helpful to someone with any control over their life, but for me, there was nothing I could do about it anyway. I didn't have the energy.

The train took a five-minute break somewhere near Stockton, and I took advantage by getting off to smoke a cigarette. When from my peripheral I saw a large man in line to board give me a slithering look. He stepped closer to me, asking for a lighter, with an awkward grin on his face, almost excited. It was the middle of the night, and I was not in the mood for flirting. I stared at the ground obviously uninterested in making small talk.

Even from a distance, I could sense something off about his vibe, but I told myself I was in no place to judge. He did, however, catch my full attention after following me into the lounge car. And neon red flags decorated the room, as he chose to sit directly next to me in a row full of empty seats.

Initially, I appeased his annoying need for chatter, and it started off like any conversation with two strangers. Until he asked me if I "liked to party." I knew that was a statement used to find out whether a person does hard drugs or not. And I picked up that he was making it known he had some, available upon request. My inability to listen to my intuition was highlighted once again. And although I knew better, I considered his offer.

Again, as I write this, I'm amazed this happened, but it wasn't the first or only time a random person offered me drugs. At the time, I was so destroyed that you could have offered me arsenic by saying it would help, and I would've taken it. My behavior chronically searching for a magical powder or pill to stop the torture of my mind. The constant circling of destructive thoughts and the questions on repeat with no answers.

After rummaging through his pocket, he pulled out and offered me a glass pipe filled with a white substance. Risking a felony and getting thrown off the train didn't stop me from taking it. With nowhere else to go, you'd think someone in my position would've made better decisions. I still can't believe I didn't catch on to the strangeness. But I took it downstairs and hit the pipe a few times, hoping it would soothe me.

Returning to the lounge car, I was caught off guard when another man began lurking nearby. The space started to feel claustrophobic even though there were only three of us there. The energy began to shift into a typhoon of darkness, choking me with dread and angst. The two men with devilish looks on their faces slowly began to flank me. I asked the new guy his name, trying to ease the tension, and he fictitiously called himself Dan.

I knew I couldn't trust them, but I played along. The Dan character had red-hair and glassy blue eyes. He swayed on his feet, licking his lips, and complimenting how pretty I was. His demeanor reminded me of a tiger restricted from its prey. Periodically shuffling towards and away from my seat as though oscillating between desire and logic. The sexual depravity in his mannerisms made the hairs on the back of my neck dance. But my thoughts were torn between anger and sadness for the mess he had become. The threshold in my rape meter had been maxed out a long time ago, and if they thought I wouldn't fight back this time, they were wrong. But I worried that it wouldn't matter in my weakened state. It never did. Within minutes I noticed more entities scattered throughout the cars that I hadn't seen before. I studied each of them looking for clues.

Manipulated Memories

Some of their faces were familiar and I thought I'd seen them following me around town but couldn't be sure. Was this the drugs or were these the people used to intimidate and keep me from talking? It felt like my existence in their game was coming full circle. All players from years of torment were present in one form or another. Was this real or was something put in the drugs to scare me, or both. I knew intuitively that the latter was more likely.

Loud music played through my clairaudient ability of Ozzy Osborn's songs. Terrifying lyrics projected by the demon collective that surrounded me. The amphetamines again amplified the psychic gifts I still didn't know I had, and I had no choice but to listen to their insidious thoughts of destruction. This distracted my ability to concentrate, making sifting through what thoughts were my own nearly impossible. From the other side of the car, I could hear the darkness inside them argue with thoughts that sounded like an evil child's fairytale. "We should gut her!" "Ya, I want to brand my name on her." "We could tie her up in the bathroom and lock the door; no one would see anything." "Pathetic human waste should be crushed!"

When I figured out that I was facing an ambush and listening to the swarms of demons who controlled them, my adrenaline kicked in. All senses kicked into overdrive. Possessed by hypervigilance and insomnia, I had no choice but to watch my worst nightmare play out in real time. Flashbacks began of when I'd seen each recognizable face. One lousy memory after the next and an internal struggle not to throw up in my seat. My escape plan disintegrated just a few hours after thinking I had gotten away. Instead, I found myself stuck in their web for the next thirty hours, going sixty miles an hour on a death train with the enemy. There was nowhere to run and even fewer places to hide. If rock bottom was a real place, it was here and now. Would I buckle, or would I fight? If there was an excuse to completely give up, this was it.

The man who gave me the drugs, we'll call Eric. He seemed to oversee the others and wanted to play good guy by signaling me to stay close to him. Unsuccessfully trying to convince me that I'd be better off with him by my side. This entire scenario changed the rules of engagement I was used to, and it surprised me. Usually, these people stayed back and threatened me from a distance. Chasing me in cars or showing weapons while walking next to me on the street. Always from a safe distance and enough room in between us that I knew that I could get away. But this, this was a firsthand level of torture that had my back against the wall. Being that he was over six feet tall and pushing two hundred fifty pounds meant I had no choice in the matter when Eric "suggested" I follow him into the bathroom. His scruffy face and dirty hands made it obvious he was a veteran meth user. Displaying black marks on the thumb and fingers from touching the glass pipe. I made a mental note that personal hygiene was not on his priority list. The smell he carried was repulsive.

Together we walked down the tiny steps into the handicapped bathroom on the first floor. Where he pulled me onto his lap and smiled, telling me not to cry. Every muscle in my body clenched and spasmed, making it hard to breathe. Malevolent energy emanated off him in an enticing and almost sexy way, which wasn't fitting for a man of his breed. He was obese and scrubby, around forty years old, with a giant handlebar mustache. His energy didn't match the profile picture. The moment he sat next to me, I trusted him with my life, and his hypnotic voice persuaded me to say things I wanted to keep to myself.

He lit up a cigarette with absolutely no care in the world. Then pulled me back on his lap as I repeatedly tried to get up. I leaned to the right to stay as far away as possible, as he said, "I'm tired of this game." Something I didn't understand. I tried to hold back a wail by grasping my palms together and squeezing my fingers till it hurt. My mind struggled to comfort me when contemplating if they would take me out right there. I was angrier about the cigarette more than anything else. Was he trying to get us kicked off the train? Was that the plan? Didn't he care that smoking on Amtrak was a federal offense? What the fuck would I do if that happened? I begged him to put it out, and he just laughed, knowing good and well he was deviously protected.

Every time I dealt with these people, I noticed the rules of this planet didn't apply. This left me to conclude that dark magic rendered them invisible to the law. He proceeded to enlighten me about what was going to happen next. That I was to be taken from the station in my hometown and "disappeared." He pulled out the meth pipe and told me it was gone, toying with me. Then threw the cig in the toilet and motioned for me to go upstairs. In a weird way, I couldn't help but appreciate that he saved the gory details about what else they had planned for me.

After this conversation, Eric wouldn't leave my side. In some sick twisted way, I didn't want him to. He was the only person giving me any information. And I yearned for answers the ones right on the edge of my vision but too foggy to make sense. Who was involved, and what were the terms? What was the goal, and was there a way out? Something was better than nothing. As I went back to my seat and curled up, holding my knees, Eric claimed the one next to me. And continually antagonized me with mind games while I stared out the window, wiping away tears.

He looked me straight in the eye and asked if I wanted to know about the times I'd been taken. All I could do was shake my head; my words were gone. He said a bunch of people raped me for hours. I could tell he was telling it as if he was there, but he had a sad look on his face. I wanted to believe he was lying but it tinged something in me, a memory I hadn't discovered yet, I could only listen in disgust.

He'd casually mention things under his breath like, "I don't want to do this," and "Maybe I can stop it," with what looked like concern on his face. But I knew it was a façade. Sometime during the ride, he made a phone call, and I could hear a female on the other end. "Do we have to do this? He asked her. "Stop being a baby!" she replied. My mind fought the effects of the drugs looking for a defense plan. But it felt like my thoughts were layered in static. Avoidance was helpful to a small degree, but I continued probing questions. Asking about the riddles plaguing my existence for decades. What was the point of my incessant targeting? Although I knew deep inside, it needed to be said aloud by someone else. Proof of the Illuminati and human trafficking. I begged for one person on Earth to validate what I'd been through.

The sun was coming up, and it was crunch time. As we inched closer to my destination, the Dan character entered a frenzy nearly foaming at the mouth, fidgeting and flailing around the isle. Eric kept ordering him back every time he crept up beside us. Five or six separate times in less than an hour. By now, every hair on my body was standing on end. My nerves were shot, and the shock of what was happening radiated through my system. Trauma from the last few nights topped with continued death threats, took a toll on my capacity to function correctly.

I noted that the theatrics on board deserved an award. When three or four of the men congregated in the back of the car to discuss technicalities and next moves, or to give high-fives and post selfies, I couldn't know. Either way, I would be left holding my sanity for dear life. While debating which was more brutal. The idea that the plan could change, and I'd be given to the madman right there on the train, was another terror I contemplated while they were away. One theory after the next of what could happen flowed through my head. Each more sadistic than the next.

Manipulated Memories

Running out of time to develop a better plan forced me to look around the area during one of their staged meetings. I staggered to the bottom floor, praying for a way out. Walking up to the emergency hatch door and pausing where a thin metal slab and red handle stood in between me and peace. I put my fist around it and tested its strength, staring at the emergency exit sign, for what felt like a lifetime. It wasn't a great idea I knew that, but it was an option. The best I could come up with. The stress urged me to pull with all my might, open and jump. It would be a final ending to the entire drama. No more terror. No more sadness. No more questions, lies, or confusion. I already knew the Source of life existed, and the divine would understand, right? A clairaudient message loudly played in my ear, "That is never the answer." I lowered my head in defeat, frustrated by that response. "What the fuck and I supposed to do then?" I asked the unknown voice. Getting no response. I trusted that they were probably right, whoever they were. And somehow, I tore myself away from what seemed like freedom and trapped myself in the bathroom for as long as possible.

Reminded by the mirror of being in the same clothes for weeks. The hits just kept coming, and I was unsure when it would end. I had let them (whoever they were) take control of my entire life, and I had to do something fast. Every stop we made gave a short-lived glimpse of hope that faded just as quickly. The drug-induced paranoia made everyone around me look dangerous. And with no money or connections, where would I go? The police were useless when dealing with my adversaries, so that wasn't an option. If the plan was to take me when I got home, I had to escape somewhere else. I decided on Portland, a familiar place and home to some family ties. But in order to move secretly, I had to leave behind every possession I had left.

A powerful surge of energy exploded through my body as I was about to exit. Pretending to go downstairs to use the bathroom, I bypassed the restrooms and scrambled off the platform into what I thought was safety on the streets of downtown. At a brisk walk I dodged the people around me, slipping into the back and then outside the front of the station, almost smiling. Until I saw Eric in the crowd waving at me with a sinister grin. He covered his head with a blue baseball cap, slid on glasses and disappeared into the crowd. My eyes darted back and forth amongst the open space desperately scanning the busy area but was unable to find him anywhere. Still in shock, and incapable of picking a direction to go in, I stood shivering outside the station, in my San Diego appropriate tank top and jeans, with no belongings or hope for hours. Searching for what to do next.

A deviant looking young man biked up to me for what seemed like no reason. Asking something irrelevant and I just squinted at him, noticing his contorted features and assessing his motives. After I didn't reply he pulled something out of his pocket and acted like he was going to hand it to me. My intuition said, "No fucking way," finally knowing better. When I didn't take it, he smiled, opening his hand to reveal a large silver and gold bullet, meant for a machine gun. He stood there for an awkward moment looking over his shoulder on both sides, and I caught site of a long handle poking out of his backpack. He dropped the bullet on the pavement next to my foot and peddled away. By that point, I was so out of it I couldn't care, I had bigger problems. I didn't even register the homeless people laughing and screeching at each other ten feet away or smell the piss and bile that littered the ground. My movements slowed and the world didn't feel real anymore. I prayed out of desperation with more emotion that I had connected to in ages, asking what the best choice was to make in this situation. Begging the Creator for mercy and requesting divine intervention.

Chapter 18

All souls are immortal but the souls of the righteous are immortal and Divine.

~Socrates

Asking someone for help was my only option. Once again, I knew cops wouldn't believe me, so I figured I'd try the next best thing, family. I knew they wouldn't trust me, but they might find compassion for my struggle. Cautiously I walked to my left, in the direction that felt best, with no plan or reasoning I could see. Thankfully, I came into the path of a short middle-aged man with grey hair and blue eyes, who asked me if I was okay. I swung my head from left to right unable to speak. "You've got to get out of here," he suggested while offering me a bus ticket good for the next two hours. I told him I needed to get to southeast, and he pointed the way. Together we waited for and got a bus headed towards my stepdads. On the ride he tried to speak to me, but my thoughts were clouded in the mystery. He looked bothered when he said out loud, "You don't remember me." I shook my head no. "Of course you don't," he replied. I knew I'd never met him, as I was always good with faces, but there was a familiarity to his essence I couldn't place.

His eyes and facial structures seemed to follow me, in different people. Just like the darkness I'd seen in Erin and Tiny except this was in a good way. Like the movie Constantine was right about the half demon and angels that walk amongst us. I'd seen others that shared his demeanor, and helpful attributes support me in life many times. At sober meetings when they said something profound, or in hospitals when they told me about my mission and how important I was. Times when nothing seemed to be going my way were littered with a usually older person that looked at me with compassion and reverence I hadn't earned. And although I did notice it in that moment, it wasn't enough to make me trust that I was gonna make it through the night. He offered me his phone, but my mind went blank. The bus stopped on the cross street towards my family's house, and I finally remembered a phone number, a dreaded call to my stepdad at the local 7-11 got me a ride and a hotel while he laughed in my face. Literally giggling at the pathetic look of me, because he thought I was out of my mind. I didn't tell him what happened, and he wouldn't have believed it anyway. I appreciated the clean space and the promise to make it home in a couple days. Considering my position, all I could muster was less than excitement to be alone in a hotel room.

I was extremely sensitive to every sound, sight, touch, taste, and smell. My body craved sleep, but emotionally I needed comfort. I called a (so-called) friend from the room, and he agreed to come the next day. But all night alone in that room, I was frightened beyond repair. I avoided the windows from the constant feeling of a red dot on my forehead. My nervous hysteria had me unable to go into the bathroom, I needed to see the entire room, or I'd panic. My bladder begged for relief, and I needed to bathe but I couldn't be in the enclosed space for more than a few seconds. I did fall asleep after a while for a couple of hours, but it wasn't enough.

Genuine fear for your life is the embodiment of chaos. No matter how often I found myself in that position, it took a long time before it got easier. I did grow less and less reactive to the threats, but my body's response each time was the same. It shut down my brain functioning for weeks. Like all the power of my electrical systems was diverted somewhere else to try and protect me. Reality became a chess game, and my friend who would show up later said it best. "You're just going to have to get creative from here." He was a precarious person who had his own understanding of mind-altering substances and dangerous people. The only kind of human fit for guiding my next moves. It's funny how valuable life experience can be, whether seemingly positive or negative, in the right circumstance.

But he was no saint and years later I'd put together that he was just another planted individual. He straight up told me he had been approached by the reptilians, describing them as humanoid looking with slits for eyes. I wasn't in the know about my life yet, so this conversation about them asking him to be an assassin went right in one ear and out the other. Which would've been valuable information once I started to trip balls for "no reason," when he came around. As I tried to distract myself by watching TV the characters were talking to me and acting out my life in brutal detail. It was terrifying but I couldn't look away. He looked at me and said, "They aren't talking to you," confused, I turned around and listened as they tore my heart out.

We left the hotel to get some food, and I noticed a foul feces smell in his car, like some had been left under his seat. The universe was trying to warn me about him. I knew what it meant but I had no one else. This was going to play out whether I wanted it to or not. When we pulled up to the hotel after dinner the front door was wide open. Nothing was taken but something was definitely wrong. After moving rooms, I stayed up all night staring at the T.V entranced by what it was showing me. He must've put something in my water when I was asleep because I wouldn't touch drugs at that point. My nervous system was stuck on, and nothing could've helped in that moment.

Looking back at this experience I can feel that his energy was the same as Tiny, Erin and a couple others I'd met along my path. Come to think of it, this exact thing happened once at Erins. These people who crept into my life as friends were never really friends. They were draconian spies and puppets, paid or forced to cause me harm. There's no doubt they were trying to make me go crazy. And come to think of it, most of those people had a blue ring around their brown eyes.

Manipulated Memories

What I learned on the train ride home could be summed up quickly. It didn't matter where I went. The danger would follow until something in me changed. After that, the choices became obvious. Either I go public or hide forever. Financially the latter was out of the question, so here I am. The main issue I face after the post-apocalyptic train ride is credibility. Once I say drugs were involved in any fashion, all accountability goes out the window. Any words after that have been met with an eyeroll and hand gesture. Each rejection of my story caused my brain to feel more like a pressure cooker than a computer, just waiting to explode. I was convinced any second could be my last and how was I supposed to combat an entire society of non-believers.

To stay safe, I phoned my sister Kayla, asking her to accept my calls but no texts because my phone had been stolen. I was grasping at straws, looking for a way to check in with someone while on a tightrope of destiny. Her being such a sweet soul, kept my language vague, trying not to scare her. She informed me of some news that, at the time, didn't make sense. And now I'm faced with even more deviousness to work out. Jera had sent out a Facebook post after she'd spoken to Damien that said I wouldn't be coming home for a while. "What the fuck are you talking about? Mom knew I was on my way there." I questioned the new information. I hadn't even seen him in weeks, and I didn't know they knew each other. Was she involved in this set up? Did my own sister help him try and get rid of me? Was she the woman on the phone on the train!? Nothing made any sense in the hurricane of fear I was in. So this detail slipped my mind for years.

The next day I finally let my body sleep, feeling secure enough with my friend around. When I woke up, I called Kayla again to check in. She claimed I'd called her an hour before and admitted I was on drugs. Not only was there no way I'd do drugs. I would never call my innocent sister and tell her I was. Part of me wants to say it was Jera who called but I couldn't prove it. Obviously, there are other options like AI but who can say for sure. These questions lingered as I went on with life. I did, however, make a mental note that the female voice I heard seemed in charge of the ambush on the train. How'd they decide to call Kayla, of all people? Was the friend with me in the room telling them what I was doing, in real time? He had to be! How did they get to everyone I knew?

Kayla thought it was odd, but I could tell she didn't buy my story either. My life felt like a bad dream, one I couldn't get out of. And no matter what I did their tactics became increasingly sophisticated. I couldn't have prepared for just how far the rabbit hole would go.

After finally getting home two days later, I stayed with my mother for a few days. She didn't understand the level of danger of the situation, and my skeleton-like appearance wouldn't allow her to. If I didn't figure something out, I was done for. My mind had been broken apart from the intensity. Sparking a new level of awareness that I couldn't have predicted in my wildest dreams. The matrix surrounding my mind ripped open and a new world began to show through. As the coding of one level of existence fell away, cracks and glitches in reality confused my eyes. And what I thought was actual magic began to happen around me. The firmament that normally shielded worlds from each other had started to disappear. The lights in the house began flickering off and on in patterns. Was something talking to me? I prayed and looked to the divine for answers, bewildered by the activity. I laid on the couch begging the Creator for sanity and strength.

Finally sober and starting to wake up, I saw that what I believed to be true never was. Nothing made sense but it did. I was no longer learning as I went, I was remembering. I began to see the connection between my vibration (thoughts and feelings) and the world's responses. Like invisible lines were being drawn from one concept to another. It started to look more like a first-person simulation game that I was somehow co-creating.

I felt like a newborn baby seeing the world for the first time, in awe of its discovery yet troubled by what it meant. Increasingly vivid dreams filled my nights, and sometimes I'd find myself lost in daydreams, exploring other dimensions. At last able to recognize that they were just as real as anything else.

This was the beginning of my journey of searching for answers from within, and the world around me started to open like a newly budding flower. I spent the majority of these days pondering existence. Something told me to think bigger. Question everything and prepare to be amazed.

Fearing for my life and desperate for safety, I checked myself into a mental health care facility after I had to leave my mom's. To be honest, when they asked me if I wanted to kill myself, I had to seriously think about it. I responded, "It would be a relief," and they decided I would stay. Had I been forced to continue this battle alone; I cannot say how long I would've survived. When I tried to tell people what I'd been through, it was met with skepticism. People would say, "I'm sorry that happened. Get over it and get a job." The world's only answer to everything. If it were that easy, I would've.

My mind tried to put together the pieces of missing time because there was an odd number of lost days in my life. Times I couldn't recall where I was or how I got there. It took a lot to discover what I was dealing with.

To handle it, my brain needed to heal. As more of the truth surfaced, I saw the actual scale of abuse, which made it even harder to believe. I couldn't help but feel like a puppet. What other people saw was not real, yet it just made me look crazy to explain it. All I could do was shrink in despair and search through the memories. I went into detective mode, ruminating for hours. Why did they spend all this time and effort taunting me? When I did start to put the puzzle together, I was baffled at how deep the scheme went.

Since you know about everything that led up to this you can't exactly see the amazing story of my awakening. Although I'll try my best to incorporate as much as I can.

But at this time, I didn't know about space, or knowing Damien and Jordan as kids. I was shocked everyday by some new detail, and just as often questioning or denying it. If I were to accept everything all at once my brain probably would've exploded.

Now I was forced to strategize on what to do next and surrender to the plan of the Creator. The only comfort was my prayers. Sitting in silence, I waited for answers. Finding a deep inner-knowing that this wasn't the end but only the beginning.

By the time I left the hospital, I felt weird itching sensations on my breastplate and an abnormal amount of faith for someone in my position, somehow, I knew everything was going to be okay. They fed us well, and finally, I was sleeping enough. I decided with the hospital that I'd go to a veteran's homeless shelter and wait for a bed in treatment. The facility was more like a low-budget apartment complex with a cafeteria. A great program run by the Salvation Army, with case managers to help us get on our feet. They gave classes to help people get housing, different spiritual groups, and even a place to get clothes. The perfect place for me to find a sense of humanity again.

When I got there, I had a deep need for something positive and uplifting. I threw myself into the shelter's program and began working in a bible study while attending events with the church and was introduced to a fun loving and gentle hearted family who took me under their wing. The wife was the first person I ever met who'd been through human trafficking too. We became close and went everywhere together. One of the very few people that witnessed the gang stalking.

Like when people would follow us on foot and act like they were waiting for a bus then jumped in a car nearby. Yelling rude comments like, "We have people watching you." She'd acknowledge them, and we'd leave, and she'd make light of the situation. Always giving me hope for a better future. Telling me she'd had similar incidents with those types of people, and they grew less interested in her over time. She assured me it'd stop and empowered me to live my best life anyway. Even then, I was too frightened to leave the building alone if I didn't have to. To deal with the stress I obsessed over my artwork, in the basement of the center.

There wasn't any real lead up to my first kundalini awakening. Just a slight sensation of energy flowing through my body, like working out hard and then sitting down quickly. The pump of my heartbeat quickened, and the circulation in my hands and feet vibrated, when my body unknowingly became able to feel the breath of the planet. As a separate inhale and exhale that showed up in a slow rhythmic flowing. Like water rushing around me. Tingling. Vibrating. Oscillating. I ignored it out of ignorance.

July 13, 2018, was the day of a partial eclipse and twelve days after my 33rd birthday. It'd become my final sobriety date for hard drugs. My heart burned and felt heavier in my chest, it pounded and pulsated, itching terribly. I put my headphones on around five pm and laid down to meditate.

Manipulated Memories

From the mothership parked above my building blasted energy waves. Entrancing the entire three-story community center to freeze in place, and time literally stopped. An unseen force paralyzed my body with a whisper, "Don't move." Many soft tranquil voices that sounded like they were on the other side of a walkie talkie, started to speak.

"Please don't worry, everything is fine. You will be on a journey to the most amazing place from now on. This is happening because you are okay with yourself. We cannot prepare you for your experience, but we are always here. We've been waiting for this day for a long time."

Then as sudden as a lightning strike, out of nowhere, a massive jolt of energy hit the back of my head. My brain folded in on itself and began turning inside out, seeming to swim in a whirlpool as my body was blasted with high frequency energy waves. My higher-self's unseen hands opened and manipulated my chakra centers one at a time up my body, upgrading my etheric systems instantly.

To my amazement, behind my eyelids small orbs grew in luminosity, morphing into animated characters and props. A large cross made of light stood in the center of the picture. Two beings walked towards it with axes resting on their shoulders and swung at the structure cutting it down. I knew intuitively it was giving me a sign to let the Christian ideology go, and I said "Okay," without resistance. Since it wasn't something, I had many feelings about, being that I wasn't raised in it. I began to levitate two feet above my bed, slowly spinning in mid-air. After my entire field was initiated, the movement suddenly stopped. Dropping my body back onto the bed so hard it knocked me out. I woke up between the wall and the bed frame with the worst neck ache of my life.

As I came to, I realized spirits and aliens were real, and they were interacting with me! They told me to do specific meditations, and each one felt like I was vibrating in water, the most blissful feeling I'd ever felt. After the activation I could feel my energy field, moving like a group of magical soft loving snakes running over my body in figure-eight patterns. It only lasted three or four days but it showed me how an energy system should feel. That one experience instantly connected me to the world of energy. Causing me to be painfully aware of people's thoughts and feelings, which at first, was overwhelming, because most of them were miserable. I could only eat raw fresh foods for the next week, after realizing everything else tasted terrible.

I took my guide's suggestions and tried my best to understand the information. But it blew my mind to be told I was a part of an ultra-soldier program and sent to Earth from a high-ranking council overseeing our universe's workings. Giant concepts, like that I'd been traveling the cosmos in different bodies and timelines to prevent certain forces from taking over. I was on the road to enlightenment, whatever that meant. An idea that resonated deeply, and I was pleasantly surprised to finally have something to live for. As I evolved spiritually, I was at the same time still being stalked by random people. They'd stop whenever they saw me, to scare me however they could. Like a homeless man who walked by a store, looked at me and loudly announced, "I have a broken bottle for you tonight."

As much as I knew I was working with beings from outside Earth, I didn't know how much they could or couldn't actually do down here, or if they were permitted to help me at all. Mostly it seems like they do small things and cheerlead me on. Which at some points was all I needed to continue.

The spiritual veil that separates worlds was weakened, and my mind expanded. I was now able to quickly grasp evolutionary ideas about the web of life and how we are all connected. I played with my new ability to give and receive loving energy to the animals in the surrounding area. Fascinated that I could feel each of them.

It was learning time.

I figured out everything I ever thought to be true was a lie. And in one day I transformed from a "normal" person to part of an awakening community of souls experiencing an accelerated evolution process. Another, much bigger timestamp for my life. I started to see the world and my relation to it very differently.

After dealing with numerous different light and dark beings, I began understanding the need for both, and yet the goal to evolve past their influence. My perception of right and wrong shifted, and black and white turned to gray. When it came down to it, being human was like playing a video game. The goal seemed to be to make enough mistakes in order to learn the best strategy to overcome the next challenge. When I learned that, everything changed. I realized I didn't go through terrible things as a punishment. All those terrible experiences were invaluable lessons that I could use to fight the bigger fights later.

In the meantime, I had to sacrifice the things I'd become attached to, including the psychological patterns handed down my family tree, or programmed as a child, to find my true self. Which would completely release me from the Matrix grid. Right now, the trauma had cracked it, and I could see a glimpse into the other side. But while still there, spiritual experiences were limited.

I aimed to find my sovereignty and set my soul free. Engaging with an existence not governed by the rules or boundaries of the physical world and trying to sit in rehab. Looking at people like they were aliens because they didn't see what I saw. Sometimes my knowings would inspire me to say things I was deeply uncomfortable with. Like giving messages to my friends from their deceased loved ones or advice to people about their life. Which seemed out of place at first, but eventually I warmed up to the idea that I was dealing with forces beyond my understanding, who were working through me.

Within months I was spirit traveling all over this world and many others, back and forwards through time, during my breaks from class. I'd meditate as long as I could, watching and feeling new universal ideas, that blew my mind. Once I became aware of the twin flame concept, I was convinced

Jordan was my other half. A reality that punctured my deep wound of abandonment.

A twin flame is a vast and complicated experience to which one opinion won't do justice. The best I can give from my innerstanding is that two aspects of the same soul come to Earth at the same time. Making available an unconditional love that supports each other's growth, even while living separate lives. That could in theory come together if that's what they agreed to, but since they're already energetically matched, they never leave each other in the other dimensions anyway. They work together unknowingly for both of their entire lives, no matter who the other one is dating or married to. Since I knew I'd come with a partner I held onto this idea and for almost five years, it crippled my ability to love anyone else. I'm not gonna pretend to know how my entire life story will end, but this potential hurt and helped me in different ways.

It caused my codependence patterns to rear their nasty heads, and I had to heal myself for years. Until finally I stopped wanting to be with him at all. I saw how much he didn't respect the value of my love for him and to be honest, he wasn't supposed to. I needed his catalyst qualities, in order to see my own value. It's kinda strange now when you think about it anyway. He's literally another version of my soul, it'd be like dating myself.

Anyone else going through this journey understands what I mean. What I want to make clear not only to you but to myself is that I have lived for eons. I've had deep and long-lasting relationships on many planets with many souls. And when I came here, I knew exactly how I was going to react to him because of the karma that'd been accrued. My guess is that it's the same for many others, and our souls use these experiences to evolve different aspects of our personalities. It really doesn't matter. He was a big, fat, giant lesson with a pretty face, and he did his job in my life well.

To all my lovesick twin flame obsessed readers. Let yourself be free from the chains of another. Love is boundless and open and available to you from many souls. Now that we're going back to the story, keep in mind that I was one of those followers for years. And that's how my soul taught me many things. I'm still open to the possibility he could someday be important to me, just no longer hung up on the idea.

Chapter 19

You will never know the power of yourself until someone hurts you badly.
~ Unknown

After leaving the treatment center, I again went back to my mother's, and my psychic gifts grew so much I was no longer able to look to anyone else for advice. I spent more and more time in the Ethers and less time around humans. It pushed me further into isolation and at times I even felt like no one else was real. It was hard to live in a world that no one else could see. I still had to exist here whether I wanted to or not, and the cycle continued, only now, it was brought to the next level.

One day in the depths of my heart, a rumbling of desperation overtook me. I was told to turn off the TV and all electronic devices. While a sick feeling and sense of panic washed over me. In front of me began to appear a story, of me standing on a spaceship having a conversation with a man who looked just like me. He held my hands tightly. "I will find my way back to you, no matter the cost. I will find you through the noise of this world." He proclaimed his love, in a matter-of-fact tone, trying to convince himself too. The sincerity in his voice broke my heart into pieces.

As I sat broken from life already, tears poured down my face and bent over my cheeks in agony. The pain of the abandonment began at my toes, clawing and clenching at every muscle on the way up my body. My stomach dry heaved from the intensity, and I couldn't help but softly groan in misery, "Oh my God." The energy of whatever dimension I was witnessing disturbed my entire system. The depth of love for this person that on Earth I barely knew was undeniable. He was me and I was him, and we were choosing to leave each other.

In order to handle the pain, I decided to take a shower. Hoping the warmth of the water would soothe my grief. Turning the knob to scolding hot I stepped in. The force of the experience prevented my ability to stand. So, I bent forward and cupped my hands around my knees. Holding myself back from screaming at the top of my lungs. It felt so wrong to see that I begged the Creator to help me. My hands trembled as the ache in my heart came in waves of vibrating suffering, with the pressure of an avalanche and I could hardly breathe. I felt myself being ripped apart, the molecules of my DNA changing from the trauma of it. Not only had I never felt this level of deep unconditional, otherworldly love before, but I felt incapable of handling the soul crushing force of its loss.

Manipulated Memories

Red angels encircled me, playing a crescendo of heavenly music. As one slowly descended in front of my vision, announcing. "Congratulations Morgan, you have passed the test of Earth. You are ready to be reunited." All around me echoed crowds of clapping and cheering, as gullible pride encompassed my being. This was the unconditional love I'd searched my entire life for. Always expecting it from others but it was only meant for one. It's what kept me going when I wanted to give up. It was the carrot on a stick in front of me that kept my hope alive, and now I realized why. It was more powerful than anything this world had to offer.

All night long I couldn't sleep, as messaging of our accomplishments played in my third eye. I watched our other lives, in awe of our adventures and dedication. Presented as a love that could change the world. The excitement had me questioning if I was ready for it. The fairy tale ending every girl dreams of. I was nervous, excited and scared. I just knew he was gonna wake up and help me save the world. Tell them about the projects, space and the hospital, and although I knew there'd be controversy, we could do anything if we were together. I considered my wedding dress and the stamp our love would have on the world. Yes, it'd seem messed up, I knew that, but we could prove that love could conquer all.

Out of the blue, Jordan called me the next day and I sprinted to an empty bedroom. My heart jumped into my throat, preparing me for the most amazing conversation of my life. My hands shook with joy as I pushed the accept button. Within seconds I could tell in his voice he was embarrassed and desperate. He needed drugs and was calling anyone he could to ask for money. I did have some, but I wasn't giving it to him for that. I'd just found out he got married right after he left me, and the pain of that news was still sore. I tried to cheerlead for him the best I could, but I was distraught over the lies of the angels. Like always, I hid my feelings and acted stoic. He said something interesting before he hung up, "Morgan, I'm not who you think I am." I chuckled and reminded him, "You're also not who you think you are." It was the best I could do to try and help him see how amazing he truly was, but his depression wouldn't allow him to believe me.

I hung up the phone and had to confront the truth that he was oblivious, indifferent and dope sick. He'd only called to beg for money. Which pulverized my heart in a way I never got over. I expected us to take on the government for what they'd done to us, or have a family somewhere tropical, but the sad truth was, I was wrong. I cried for hours, struggling to breathe in between devastations, curled in a ball on my mom's bed. Every cell in me begged for someone to hold me, but the silence that met my cries was deafening. No one could relate to what I was engulfed in. How could they? This wasn't some high school crush who chose someone else. This was me abandoning myself, and the weight of it rebounded off the loveless walls. It was no use; it was out of my control. My mind couldn't compute the brutality of it, and I sat questioning everything. "How could someone forget something so strong? Why would they ever want to? Why did

Manipulated Memories

I come here to be tortured like this!? Laughter surrounded me, along with hisses and rudeness. "You thought you were done! It's only the beginning. It gets worse from here. He doesn't love you. No one does. Poor Morgan, sad, helpless, pathetic."

Until I sensed Jordan connecting with someone else, giggling and whispering, then making love. Tears fell in between my spurts of rage. "What the fuck is going on! Why am I being forced to watch this? How do I turn it off!?"

It was obvious now that the crowds were legions of fallen angels. On a mission to help me heal the deepest abandonment I'd ever felt, by tearing the wound open in a way that only they could. It'd take another five years before I told him I'd been in love with him since the day we met. There's no way from my actions he could've put that together. He was surprised when I finally came clean, but it'd been too long to fix all the pain. He didn't want me anyway, he wanted literally anyone else but me at that point, and I couldn't blame him. The heartbreaking truth is maybe he never will. What if he never remembers our mission? What if he doesn't care when he does? These questions surrounded me for years, as I was shown his life, his loves, and his children. What if this simulated reality takes over his understanding? What if he likes the Matrix so much that he'd rather stay here? Choosing the girl in the red dress over the truth.

I've never felt so out of control about something in all my life. I could usually get my way if I wanted something, but this was soul contract stuff. Something that even fate couldn't change, and to top it off, I had a front-row seat to his world, and I couldn't tell him. We were so connected that his energy came up just as often as mine did, in my dreams and visions. I begged for it to stop, sometimes angry, others sad. One day turned into a month turned into years and kept on running. A show of possibilities I couldn't rewind or fast forward. One situation after the next of annoying details.

In this reality, I opted to steer clear of him altogether. We talked on the phone a handful of times, and once or twice I tried to explain who I was to him, but he ignored me. I also told him about knowing he was a part of the rapes with Damien, but I was so chickenshit I took it back. When it came to Jordan there wasn't anything normal about the way I acted. And although it drove me crazy, I couldn't help but wait for the day he made good on his promise. Until I was so fed up with it, I closed that door for good. Allowing me to finally fall in love with someone else.

A few weeks after the false reunion, I scrolled through spiritual YouTube and saw a video on walk-in souls. Something about the topic piqued my interest and I watched many like it throughout the day. Later that evening, my soul taught me to open portals by suggesting hand gestures and intentions. I played with opening passageways in between the Earth and Etheric realms unaware of its power. My spiritual ignorance didn't know how to close them, and the energy around me fell dark quickly, as density poured through the gap in the veil. A heavy feeling filled the house, and I held on for the ride.

Manipulated Memories

My mother didn't notice the change and wasn't one to talk about the Source of life or magic. We sat watching a movie with her normal uninterested demeanor, and I didn't say anything because she would've scoffed at the idea. After the show ended, she went to bed but in the middle of the night she awakened, flustered and bothered. Coming out to the living room and startling me awake; to tell me something had told her to meditate, and that she thought she'd left her body. She sat outside smoking cigarettes for a long time and came back in and went to bed. I was actually excited about what she'd said and went back to sleep hoping she'd be awakening too. What a cool thing it'd be to have a mother with something to bond over. Intuitively I knew that'd be a stretch, but my idealist naivety still knew no bounds.

Within hours I heard her rustling and trampling through the house in a quiet panic. I crept towards her bedroom door and saw her shoving items into a trash bag. I watched the insanity on her face for minutes, searching for what was wrong with her. Questioning my spirit team but they didn't respond. My body was sluggish from the intensity of the darkness, and I felt helpless. As time dragged on, I asked her what she was doing. Her voice sounded foreign as she replied, "Getting rid of everything of value." I looked at her in shock as she piled her jewelry, boots, shoes and expensive purses together. "Why?" I questioned her. "I don't need them anymore," a response that sent chills down my spine, because I knew my mom wouldn't do that. She coveted those things. I sat on the couch confused and watched. The discomfort was consuming and the only relief I found was in a short message from the Ethers, "This is meant to happen." It was an answer, but not a clue.

I joined her outside to smoke in between rants, trying to gauge what her motives were, but she just frantically played on her phone. I couldn't sense her energy anymore, and the more she spoke the less I saw of my mother. That theory had me avoid her for the rest of the morning as she threw the bags outside, rambling nonsense and her love for Jesus. It felt like I was in a horror movie. What the fuck was she talking about? She'd never once talked about religion of any kind. And since when does Christianity say anything about not having jewelry or nice clothes?

I finally called Jera and told her the parts of the story she could handle. She was pissed she had to be involved since she had to work the next day, but she did help me get her to the hospital by calling the authorities. She thought our mom was having a mental breakdown, but I knew better. Our mother was gone. While she sat in the hospital, I closed the portal and made plans to leave town, but I still only had the four hundred bucks the VA was giving me. Thankfully mom called from the inpatient center and told me to use her credit card if I needed it, so I bought stuff to travel with.

My last resort of safety had just been removed. I was terrified to be on my own, but this was happening whether I wanted it to or not. When she returned, she took her stuff out of the shed and brought it back in the house. Saying she felt better now, but I could see through my gifts that the being inside her wasn't human at all. The Christianity talk only worsened and overnight she said she had become "Born again." "Ya, I guess that's one name for it," I chuckled to myself. She obsessed on her phone, and being my curious self, I made sure to catch a glimpse of what she was doing. I saw weird writing that didn't make sense, but I didn't say anything. I was already so freaked out that I didn't want to know who she was now. She was less bothered by life, which was good, and even gave me a ride to the bus station to go live with a random lady near Sedona, that I'd found on a craigslist ad.

The next few months were spent traveling from one city to the next every couple weeks, trying to stay clear of my stalkers, but somehow they kept finding me. I knew to stay away from Damien but hadn't put together his involvement yet.

Now it was late 2018, and I was hiding from him in a hotel, pondering my options. Closing my eyes when spirit let me know through my spidey senses, it was time to meditate. I paused my YouTube video and laid on the bed. My heart rate calmed, and my mind slowed. Each inhalation grew heavier. I relaxed as the darkness behind my eyelids cleared into my inner galaxy. Right away, I felt conflicted after I sensed a connection between two people, I didn't think knew each other. Damien and Jordan. I watched in awe as time moved backwards, by moving my attention. And into a scene of the last time I saw Jordan in person. When he'd insisted, I come to that small gathering. At first, I felt disappointed in my past decision and winced, embarrassed by my neediness. After a moment I forgave my poor choices and continued on with the story. Drawn to when he was in the bathroom. I was pulled into the room to learn the secrets of a lie so callus, it had me question my sanity. Inside the literal closet was a man waiting for Jordan. A man who chose that scenario as a joke. A mean malicious twisted game. My ex-Damien.

I lunged forward, slamming my fists on the bed, while standing up in protest. "No fucking way," I shouted out loud. In the silence of the room, I listened to my heart pounding while my entire body began to tremble. Did I just see what I think I saw? My mind began to race with controversy, as a vortex of energy spun around me. "They live two states away from each other. There's no way they could've just met randomly. What the fuck is going on!?" My eyes sank into detective mode, and I laid back down, determined to find out more.

I was transported to the moment after hearing rustling and noticing the lights were off in the bathroom. I watched myself knock on the door. As Jordan opened it, he was glistening with sweat. A byproduct of the stimulant ring of white powder dripping from his nostril. With my obsessed ignorance, I stepped inside and shut the door behind me, and again, we kissed and had sex. As the reenactment played, I moved around the circumference to see the room from all directions. And Damien's silhouette appeared watching through the slats in the small closet door, pleasuring himself to our interaction. Wrath poured through my veins as I began to understand what spirit was trying to show me. They planned this, and every person in that house knew about it. I was a fool, again.

Damien knew I'd fallen in love with Jordan, and this was his revenge. I kept moving through that evening's events looking for clues. Scouring for deception as Jordan caressed my ego and asked me to be his girlfriend, as he held my hand on the rooftop. Combing through his mannerisms and movements, as he sat down, and I sat in between his legs. I mumbled something vulgar about his acting skills in a sassy tone, as I saw him holding me from behind and kissing my neck. The rage boiled my blood to remember how blissfully unaware I'd been at the time. A deception that'd made me the happiest delusional girl in the world.

After reviewing more evidence of the story, and unable to watch anymore, I jumped up from bed, furious. Uncontrollably pacing my hotel room from end to end. "How could I have been so stupid?" I said aloud to the universe. Heavy tears poured down my cheeks as I sat on a chair and grabbed a cigarette. The more I put together the pieces of why these types of things happened, the less Jordan and Damien seemed responsible. It started to look like they were puppets, used to do the dirty work others couldn't be seen doing themselves.

On the surface, they'll look like type-A alpha thugs but they were told what to do and when to do it. And although they didn't have to act on those impulses, they did. Yes, as we all do, they had choices, but they were set up in ways they couldn't comprehend. It took years of watching their story before I finally accepted it was true. Only after, I went back and forth, trying to convince myself it wasn't. A secret connection that would cause the downfall of many.

After I learned about this event, their connection became obvious. Jordan would call me the same day Damien would, but never any other time. And the last time I saw Damien; I noticed someone named Jordan was calling him. He stood frozen in shock and didn't know what to do. So, I got angry and said I knew what was happening, but he ignored me.

Recently, I learned that I had a type. Younger men who secretly hated women and were attracted to the darker side. A clear pattern in my disaster of relationships track record. I tried different tactics to get them to admit it. Even allowing Damien over to my hotel a year later, if he'd agree to sign a confession about his involvement in the rapes. Hoping to get him to admit to everything. When he got there, he appeared so guilt-stricken he did it without confrontation. I was too chicken shit to ask about Jordan though, I was terrified of the answer.

Fearing for my safety, behind his back, I called the police. They took the statement but couldn't take him to jail after he lied and said it wasn't true. Another point when the cops could've saved me from years of struggle. But they asked me if I wanted to put him in jail, and I couldn't say yes. I knew deep down it wasn't his fault, and it would've been impossible to explain that to them. They already looked at me like I was insane for my past mistakes, and it would've been ridiculous to tell them scientists made him do it. So, I just asked them to force him to leave. The next day he sat outside my room, begging to come in anyway.

That experience watching the boys was one of the first looks into the lives of the people I loved. Before that, my gifts were being tuned and teaching me about universal laws. Now I dreaded the thought that I could see the past, present, and future. It felt like a life sentence to something I never wanted. An inescapable front-row seat to the treacheries and deceptions from all directions.

Until then, I'd enjoyed the ignorance of believing everyone was a good person. Regardless, I'd be rocked to the core by the reality of the people's intentions in my life. Every time I closed my eyes, I was met with friends, family members, and exes getting together and plotting my demise.

The first big shock about the multiverse was that every single moment of all life is recorded, and available for inquiry from anyone with my gifts. That had me uncomfortable for days. Floods of embarrassment and shame overcame my senses as I remembered all the idiotic things I'd done that I thought no one would ever know. Every booger picking and shower or lack thereof, every sex scene, every thought. Every mental breakdown and self-pleasuring. Every heartache and infidelity. Not to mention the unspeakable sexual fantasies. All alive and immovable inside the quantum field. I wasn't spared from the gossip sessions my closest friends and family members had about me either.

Manipulated Memories

Some days I'd be watching a movie, and a string of conversations would play in my mind, and I could feel who they were from their energy imprint (like a fingerprint). I knew it was karma for the same thing I'd done to others, so I couldn't be mad.

At first it was brutal to hear my ex's talk about how terrible I was in bed, or how I didn't shower or brush my teeth long enough. It became comical as ridiculousness came out of the mouths of my sisters, mom, dad and friends. And it had me understanding just how silly I sounded talking about the behaviors of other people. Gossip is a toxic slime, oozing off the people who partake in it. Its stench seeping through their pores, attracting more of the same.

I saw that people's behavior has a reason that we aren't always privy too, and since no one is free from misbehaving, it doesn't matter if it makes us feel good to spill the T. It has long lasting traumatic effects when those conversations become the subjects self-talk. Learning that stopped that action in me, real fast. I saw just how right Jordan Peterson was when he said, "No one gets away with anything, ever."

Ready or not, I was on a one-way road to Truth-town. Behind my eyelids and through my third eye, I watched short films one after the next without a remote. Heartbreak after heartbreak, sometimes for days. Until I couldn't shed another tear, and all that was left was forgiveness. I didn't sleep well for months as I feared closing my eyes. But there was no getting away from my spiritual destiny, and I would have to open my eyes to relax my mind.

Chapter 20

Everyone is jealous of what you've got, no one is jealous of how you got it.
~ Jimmy Carr

In my regular meditations, I was shown my missing time in baby spoonfuls, because I was already barely hanging on as it was. Starting with working through the Mk-ultra stuff, like the times I'd been taken from school or gymnastic practices. And driven to a secure location, seeing Damien and Jordan there, which threw my head for a loop. I was already doing the best I could just to get through the day, so at times it felt surreal and unbelievable. Especially when they showed me that some of the kids in my regular elementary and middle school were planted there. Their entire families were working for the projects, and we'd get close (usually over gymnastics) and I'd be able to stay with them for the weekend. Which is when I would end up at Elitest.

Then came the memories of the missing days with Damien as an adult. It was hard to keep up with and I was frustrated that the story didn't present itself in chronological order. The quantum field didn't care about what I wanted to see. The information that was most important for me to know was what was going to be available. I'll talk about how that is regulated later. One by one, the stories of the rapes surfaced. Piercing my identity with uncertainty. I knew Damien was wild but there was no way I could've been prepared for what I saw. The more I watched, the more the boys' club started to look like a well-organized and funded ring of individuals. Some of the events looked facilitated by government officials, or the projects themselves. Here's one example of why I came to that conclusion.

One of the nights with Damien, he handed me a drink of soda laced with a sedative, and I fell asleep with it in my hand. He first raped me on his own and then called over a group of six men. Who while speaking slander and spitting on my face, stuffed my body into a large duffel bag and threw a layer of clothes on top. Four of the people grabbed a handle strap and carried the bag down the apartment stairs. As a precaution, I was thrown into the trunk already filled with other identical bags. It was clear someone had planned this, and it looked surprisingly professional.

Two cars followed behind as the original proceeded down the freeway heading towards the Mexican border. After crossing it with only a quick look through the bags, my body was taken down a back road somewhere in Tijuana. Where the group was met by a truck similar to a military Praga V3S (a cargo-hauling vehicle). Once they both made it to the destination I was removed and tossed in the back. Damien and Jordan sexually pleased each other while I bounced around on the metal bed. We pulled up to a house in the middle of nowhere, where I was taken inside.

The boy's hand-washed my privates and set me in a chair alongside six other women, all asleep. Headphones were placed on our heads, and subliminal messages shoved into our brains.

"You will never tell anyone about this. You are scum and worthless. No one loves you. You are only suitable for sex," Different phrases of damnation played into our minds.

Each one of us were then individually taken into another room filled with groups of men and Damien's sex swing connected to the ceiling. One by one each girl was placed on, and videotaped while being assaulted. Before dawn, a pile of money was handed to Damien and Jordan for bringing us in, and the girls were loaded back onto the truck and taken to a small river nearby. While unconscious, we were thrown into the rushing water! Jordan jumped in and pulled me to the shore just before I drowned, because he knew Damien would be the first person the cops looked at if something happened to me.

To be honest I think the boys were switched into their other soldier identities. On some occasions I want to say they weren't and on others, like this one, they very well could've been. Which means they don't remember doing this at all. Which puts an entirely different spin on the game we were in. You'll have to ask them; I doubt they'll be speaking to me much after this.

Manipulated Memories

Together they placed me back into the duffel bag and prayed to Satan the border police wouldn't find me. Driving back to California must've been terrifying with such precious cargo, and this time they were ordered out of the car while being searched. But once again the cops magically didn't open the bag I was in.

As these memories came up, I was forced to see the level of darkness inside them. While dating, I would've never believed either one could've done these things, I thought they loved me. I finally understood why the girl who came to Damien's apartment asked to see me. I wasn't just a joke to them, I was a toy, an oblivious lovesick puppet.

The people they worked with had obviously been doing this for years and had their evil down to a science. They picked the girls no one would take seriously and used drugs to keep them knocked out. Making it hard to prove, but if the cops look, they'll find something I'm sure of it.

The shame of this experience was ego-crushing, but quite honestly, I felt sadness for my persecutors. After learning about the karma they've acquired, I'm genuinely sorry for their souls. Each one has no idea what they've gotten themselves into. I've seen that even in death, they won't escape what they've done, and they'll pay for these atrocities one way or another.

They will try to say I've always been crazy, and my life was definitely set up to ensure they'd have that argument. Don't give in to their control tactics; decide for yourself. Could I have made this all up? I never wanted to be a writer.

Manipulated Memories

As you saw, I didn't make it past the tenth grade. I only wrote this to try and protect the children still in these programs and get the world to look at the VA Hospital in La Jolla. A place I'm sure still traffics girls today, because no one will ever know without someone coming forward. I'm not naive to how dangerous this is, but if no one else will talk about it, then I have to.

The reason this type of thing is able to continue is that there's been a deception on this planet facilitated by both false light and dark beings. Who perpetuated the idea that seeing is believing. The drive for scientific study and the need for physical proof has kept the masses stuck in a third-dimensional understanding. What people fail to realize is that it works quite the opposite. If someone doesn't believe, they will not see. The mind can't override the belief system. I now have deep empathy for humanity, because they know not what they do. The only job everyone NEEDS is full-time spiritual development. To get them past the preconceived notion that the physical world can prove anything.

My masculine higher self (which is not another entity, it's just me) offered to prove he was real to me in a dream. As I was awakened from sleep, he asked if I wanted him to play with my hair or scratch my back, and I said the latter. As I opened my eyes, he gently ran his nails across my skin as I lay awake. Which brought faith back to my lonely world. I was renewed with the hope that everything was going to be okay, because I was no longer (if ever) doing this on my own. And now I had tangible evidence that I wasn't just crazy.

Manipulated Memories

I learned that what I went through was all based-on frequency, that'd been manipulated early on. I put together multiple experiences where people were literally drawn to me. Whether that was good or bad depended on how I was feeling. When paranormal things happened, I was so excited I told everyone. Which didn't go over well. I was aware of things people around me couldn't grasp, and eventually I'd learn not everyone wants to know. In the early days, my information was either unfounded or unwanted and never taken seriously. It was just too early in my journey to explain what I saw to others.

It was often disheartening to see people walk around with their consciousness asleep. I learned very quickly that that's how it's supposed to be. It didn't occur to me until later that everyone's life is designed that way. The fact that people cannot understand spirituality is not because they don't want to. On the contrary, it's perfectly orchestrated and preplanned to give them the opportunity to find it on their own.

As my mind upgraded over the next couple of months, I could see myself maturing and releasing emotions on command. Slowly my ego let go of its death grip on my psyche, and it was fascinating to see how it affected me. Controlling everything I did and comforted only by staying in my usual patterns. As I chose to heal my inner child and release blocks in my energy fields, I literally felt lighter. Slowly I gained control over my emotions and thoughts.

Manipulated Memories

Every day I was having new fantastical spiritual adventures. Like seeing energies in the air that looked like holographic glass silhouette shapes. I'd lay in the grass and stare at the sun to see the parts of another world. I'd have to squint and concentrate as hard as I could to make out the beings made entirely of light. A magic beyond words with swirling colors and unidentifiable patterns and shapes. A world different in every way from our own. The more I released my negative emotions, the clearer my clairvoyant screen got, and it's simpler than you may think. I see into the quantum realms. The worlds of spirit that are all around us all the time. Too small or too big to see with the naked eye.

When I processed the information, it came in two parts. Intellectual data and emotional memory. Emotional memory was stored in my body's energy field on the quantum level, and the intellectual data was what was blocked from my conscious mind, from the machine's. But the emotions never healed unless I consciously made the effort to, so they were all still intact. I see them as segmented mini-plays, in my personal field, in between worlds where the physics are changeable depending on which one I'm watching. Each one living right next to us but seeming so far away. I learned time doesn't exist in between dimensions/planes, and that everything that's ever happened or will ever happen is happening now there. Which is how I can see the past and future. I maneuver myself through timelines and witness what my soul feels is beneficial for my growth.

Manipulated Memories

The world will want to say they are hallucinations. But I've experienced both and know the difference. In that way, my psychotic episodes were a blessing. I may've never been able to trust my visions without witnessing the differences firsthand.

It's not a metaphor when they say that the eyes are the window to the soul. The more I aligned my chakras and purged, the more I was shown. The first full spirit I ever saw up close was my old family dog. She was young, happy, healthy, and excited to see me, which was incredible.

The possibilities are endless in the spirit realm. I could speak with deities and spiritual leaders or my guardian angel, which was no big thing. Something they want me to help others understand is that they're not above us. Angels, guides, and all spiritual deities are not better than you or I. They're our brothers and sisters. Even the highest of other-dimensional beings want you to consider them friends and equals. This world wants to put what they don't understand on a pedestal. But they got to where they are in the same way you did.

I began to study astrology relentlessly. Learning about the different aspects of myself changed my perspective on why my life was the way it was. My birth chart enlightened me in ways nothing else could've. Giving me clear practical guidance on how to pursue my future. I recommend this spiritual tool to absolutely everyone. Please look at the metaphysical map that you chose to experience in this world. Dive deep into the world of astrology, and you'll not only understand yourself, but use it to support your life. While teaching you about your friends, family members, and partners. Let me be clear about something though, just because astrology is a real energetic map that a soul uses to guide it through its past karma. Doesn't mean it's a life sentence. There are ways to evolve through the birth chart and beyond the good verse's bad concepts, once a person has come to complete neutrality and then holds a frequency of love. Past the karmic field and into a world of joy for no reason, gratitude beyond measure every day, and fulfillment without greed. All is available to those who seek.

There are phases to this enlightenment process, and some days I felt connected to every living entity, including the planet. I'd vibrate so high that I felt like a floating giant ball of love, and nothing could bother me. And the very next day, get an 11,000$ bill in the mail, and it was back to square one. Pizza and beer.

I was meditating for hours a day now, doing no other activities, only focused on spiritual growth. Thus began the harder side of ascension. To my dismay, there were many days when my energy body would float an inch or two above my physical one. I'd have to sit or lay for hours as I couldn't walk or sleep without feeling like I would fall through the floor. Fear of leaving the body and being unable to come back made this mentally difficult. But trust me when I say that's not how it works. Once I learned that meditation strengthened my connection to my soul, the more time I spent in the Ethers, traversing the underworld for the next couple of years. A vast space filled with every mistake and fear created since I was born. Where I found the answers to my authenticity. Darkness has its place and needs to be respected. We wouldn't be the people we are without it.

Behind the veil of evil is a vast land filled with crystalline structures. Buildings made entirely of colored light that shimmer like glass. The contrast between the pitch black and sparkling colors is a sight I wish all to have. But it takes the ability to walk through the fire of worst fears without judgment, and into your kingdom of sovereignty. A journey not many can make.

I'll do my best to give you an idea of what some of my visions looks like. When I close my eyes, initially I see a world of light that in the beginning was a jumbled mess of memories. After years of the healing process a bridge between my conscious and subconscious mind was uncovered. On either side dwelled reflections of events I hadn't thought about since they happened. Density and distress that held me down until I did.

As the astrological world rotated it brought new experiences into my awareness. Scenes of myself with other people or alone doing particular activities. As I moved past and come to one that needs to be healed, it unfolds as if it's happening again. The remnant feelings well up in my stomach and release through my tears.

Once I became more familiar with the process, I could transmute the dense energy into love using alchemy. Some memories are beautiful moments I miss; others are tragic endings I wished never happened. All stuck in my body like boulders on a highway. I couldn't progress until a certain amount was healed. One by one, I explored my past and watched the future possibilities. I know this almost sounds dreamy, but seeing yourself in this light can be challenging. The only consistent thing about the spirit realm is that it's made up of several dimensions and levels. Some of which are the same except for trivial details. In order to evolve at the pace I wanted to, I had to reach an energetic threshold, which went on for hundreds of hours.

This process was how I found out about the hidden traumas. It would've been impossible to put together without this gift, and I'm genuinely grateful for it, and it was a grueling process that took years and didn't shut off when excruciating. Every time I closed my eyes; I was met with the truth. On the worst days, I held my head crying, swaying back and forth, begging for it to stop.

On the best days, I was shown the multi-verse and the physics that governs it. Watching my past god lives and learning where my neurosis came from. Which gave me the strength to change those behaviors, and sometimes I got to bask in the light of Source and regain my love for all.

But most days, I trudged the underworld. People call it the Dark Night of the Soul. And the way it plays out in the 3D realms is that life gets difficult. Most humans don't know what's going on and chalk it up to bad luck. I on the other hand had to see it before it manifested. I watched the struggle from the field as my Soul transversed the darkest parts of my psyche, as well as the collectives. Planes of existence that were filled with fear, sadness, guilt, shame, anger, envy, and lust. Either underwater, on land, or in the sky. The things I saw are beyond words. But one example would be, thousands of people floating in water, eating each other alive, having sex, and morphing into creatures at the same time. It was worse than any scary movie you could imagine, and I was bewildered by the level of wickedness.

Something to keep in mind when we deal with creatures of the darker realms like demons, is that they work for the light. The balance of good and evil is a delicate perfection, and they have a purpose. We experience the existence of these beings both inside and outside of us to become stronger. Without these interactions would we learn anything? I doubt it.

It's their job to come up with evil masterminded plans and they do what they're meant to do. I know the world is terrified of these beings, but that's the whole thing! Don't be. They can't win if you don't let them.

Once people realize they can heal negative thoughts instead of believing them, the power will shift in a better direction. But both sides of the spectrum come with challenges. The love and light or good vibes only idea creates the potential for spiritual bypassing, a naïve paradigm that's dangerous. Delusional misconceptions that teach people to ignore the darkness within. Which can implode/explode all over their lives if they let it. There's no way to skip the healing journey of ascension. If someone does, they're asking for an entirely different can of worms.

Manipulated Memories

I will say, the density of the dark realms did come with unpleasant physical symptoms. Nightmares and hauntings made it hard to sleep. Intense, heavy energies poured down on me, sinking me into depression for months. It was such an interesting contrast to be witnessing amazing magical adventures and yet feel helplessly alone in it. Even while interacting with beings from the other side.

I became more isolated as my gifts got stronger, because I couldn't explain what was happening to me to anyone. When I tried, they snubbed their nose or ignored it, and I began to feel like no one would ever understand. I had no choice but to stay to myself. I didn't know who I could trust anyway. Fear told me everyone was a possible spy. Which caused me to retreat into myself and neglect my human life. Barely doing the minimum to survive.

Food became a weapon of my stress, and I was either eating raw vegetables or entire pizzas. I used my bulimia to have some sense of control during a wildly uncertain portion of life. The spiritual ego I had created wanted me to be a perfect vegan and would demean me if I ate anything else. And the rebel within me hated rules so much that it went back and forth eating as much junk food as possible. Then I'd work out for hours a day to make up for the food. It wasn't a pretty picture, but it was one that I hid well.

Watching spiritual videos about fasting and high vibrational diets didn't help my situation. People who don't know what they are talking about when it comes to food should really watch what kind of content they put out. You never know what someone is going through. I tried fasting and my ego loved it. I was tortured and miserable so the sabotaging part of me was satisfied. But when I returned to eating, I ate till I got sick. Not everyone needs to fast, and for some of us it's actually harmful.

What I learned later through trial and error is that once the body is done with a certain type of food, it will no longer taste good. There is no reason to force yourself to eat things or not eat other things because of some diet or spiritual b.s. The source of life doesn't ask for suffering in return for anything, it's just that this world is convinced that it does.

My body rejected hard drugs so much that I couldn't do them even if I wanted to, and since I was still plagued with PTSD, I looked for other substances to soothe me. Weed helped for a while but didn't last after I started floating from even the CBD alone.

You can bet, I had many temper tantrums as these forced changes occurred. I'd stomp my feet and say, "I've been through so much, I deserved to have something to help me feel better," but it was no use, and there was no one to blame. My body was being upgraded and toxins weren't handled well anymore.

Kratom became my new best friend. A substance that was natural enough I could handle taking it for about five years after my awakening. Would you guess that I became just as addicted to it as the others. It'd become a part of my personality at that point to lean on something, and honestly, I don't judge myself for it. The immense task of rewatching my life was the hardest part of this experience. I'm glad I had something that gave the illusion of comfort even though it didn't really do much to ease me.

The more my consciousness grew, the better I was able to understand other dimensional life. I learned about unique utopian worlds where negativity doesn't exist at all. My dreams became more real than waking life, and sooner than later, I could control them. My life truly had become like a movie.

I want to clarify a couple of things on divination and magic. After seeing what's happening in the Etheric realms, I learned the hard way not to mess with it. People need to be careful. Dark beings can use crystals and tarot cards to bring in bad luck. Once you know you are strong enough, they can be used to support your life. But I don't recommend any of it until you know what you're dealing with, if ever, it's completely unnecessary.

Over time this emotional rollercoaster brought me to my knees. Then built me back up, just like the Army. I had to release and give up everything I knew, to make room for the bigger picture. This was compounded by my ego wanting to stay precisely where it was. Always urging me to give in to temptation. Sometimes, I'd use my setbacks as failures and plunge myself into self-pity and blame. Cursing at the universe and my guides for not handing me the success they promised. I was impatient and bratty, I wanted what I wanted, and I wanted it now. The more I resisted, the worse it got. What I refused to understand was that I couldn't control anything except myself.

One day, after having a long pity party with negative responses to everything. My guides took my astral body on a journey to hear and feel what other people were going through, when I laid down for a nap. I was pulled out of my skin and hovered through the world. Taken to people in hospitals with their families, and then to see arguments and sad thoughts people were having about their futures. Showing me firsthand that other people were struggling too and that I wasn't alone. Everyone like me, goes through this in their own way. Not that our experiences are the same, but the impact on our lives is. We must be taken to the point of no return. A place where we can shed our negative beliefs and build new ones.

I needed to stay grounded and keep my eyes on the prize of peace. This was no easy feat, and I assure you that anyone on this journey is an absolute miracle. The devastation of these events cannot be put into words, and the only thing that will help us through this is self-compassion.

These things that happened to me shouldn't even be possible. Yet they happen all over the world every day. Ranging from domestic violence to slavery. What can I say to people who've lived through this sort of thing?

Only that Earth is a co-creative multidimensional sacred heroic tournament. A holographic arena where we play out our deepest desires and darkest fears. It isn't personal. How people behave is part of a bigger pattern, cemented when they were very young. Even if someone spits in your face, it isn't about you, they're doing it to themselves, no matter what it looks like.

Most people don't know that everyday people worldwide are waking up to their spiritual nature. More of them seeing and feeling these alternate realities. While opening new levels of consciousness that allow for a deeper awareness. Teaching them who they are and why they're here. For everyone, the path is different, but the goal the same. Find peace, serenity, and joy in a world full of chaos.

As I healed each chakra center, it caused more alchemical changes to my DNA. Allowing me to upgrade my physical body and ascend my consciousness. I met my over soul in the twelfth dimension a couple of weeks ago and found out we are a creator goddess that protects worlds. She stood taller than the entirety of the cosmos, and it was hard to grasp how that was possible. Our aura felt ancient and powerful beyond words. She hung suspended and incorporeal in between universes. With no face or determined features, only an outline that appeared human for my benefit. And although there are a million silly teachings about the Higher Self, Soul, Over Soul and Source consciousness…I want to make one thing clear. There's no separation between any of them! They're not beings that live in the clouds you need to connect to. It's all you.

I keep referring to consciousness and you may ask, what is consciousness exactly? This has been debated since the beginning of time, but I'll give you my view. It's the observer of the human experience. It watches our thoughts and emotions and then makes the decisions. It's our true self, unbridled Source/Creator energy. It holds the capacity to intake divine information. That creates the person's depth of awareness of the self and connection to others. It's the one thing responsible for the ability to love and accumulates lifetimes worth of growth and expansion into usable knowledge. The DNA is a computer code that collects and stores that data. Our bodies are quantum computers deciphering the information.

The answers to my biggest questions came when I was able to find the patterns. That the relationships I had with my family, replayed with every person I ever met. Just noticing that allowed me to step onto a higher timeline. Which in turn allowed me to see more patterns. Like dating the same people who I met in the same way. Even the sexual assaults were all connected, because they started when I was a child who was helpless to stop them. Then continued and escalated into being drugged over and over.

All the way to the eating disorder that weaved its way through my life, starting from my relationship with my mother. Every trouble in my life was a part of a puzzle held together by invisible strings of similarities. Creating a web of misinformation that I needed to take down. When I saw the connection consciously, the habitual subconscious programming stopped in its tracks. Healing not only the ancestral karma but my personal as well. Until I was able to be present, not worried about the future, or the past, and every moment felt like a peaceful eternity. Anxiety was gone, and depression couldn't hold me down any longer.

After these patterns became glaringly obvious, so did the understanding of my part in it. I wasn't some helpless victim to a harsh world. I was the creator of it. I was although oblivious still responsible for every single act that'd been placed upon me, and that pill was hard to swallow. It wasn't the rapes, or stalking that tortured my mind, it was my responses to them. It wasn't the eating disorder or the drug addiction that ruined my life. It was me, and it wouldn't be anyone else who'd fix it.

Running from the boys, Tiny's friends and the projects only fueled the fire. So, I had to stop, turn around and say something. I learned that although spirit guides my path, I have the choice to listen or not, and sometimes I'm not supposed to.

When all is said and done, I had to trust myself, and that was scary. I was wrong about so many things. I had lists of reasons not to. You reading this have them too. But what if the reason those things happened in the first place was because I didn't trust myself from the beginning. I know you saw the day that changed for me when I was five, but the responsibility is still mine. And the only way to change the future is by doing it differently.

I've realized that the real reason we're here isn't to build houses, get a million followers, or make a certain amount of money. It's about finding ourselves, and being initiated into other dimensions of love. Where we can interact with other aspects of ourselves that want to show us a better way. Once our mind opens to the possibilities of magic and wonders, we are free to experience them. By becoming limitless beings free to roam the cosmos with just a thought. While also living in a 3D reality. With its amazing physical senses that don't exist in other realities. We can have the best of all worlds.

It's sad most people don't know what they're missing, and yet, if they did, they'd be miserable they couldn't have it. So, I understand why people can't accept the truth of afterlife/beforelife. It'd crush them to know just how beautiful and terrifying it can be.

As I write about my whimsical journeys through the Etheric waters, I sit in a bedroom just like yours. I open my laptop and complain that it's eighty degrees at ten a.m. in October, in Vegas, like anyone would. I take a shower and get ready to play a human character, just like you. I deal with all the same things like bills, classes and continued struggles with behaviors I wish to change. And I say that to remind you that you can have what I have.

This part of the multiverse is heavy. The emotions and trauma we experience are impossible to describe without tears. Yet I'm here to tell you that you were built to handle it, and everything that goes with it. You are the MVP and strongest version of you that's ever existed. One day you'll find that out, when you're on the other side of the pain.

Your higher self is not your highest self. That lives within you.

Manipulated Memories

And every person on this Earth whether you like, agree with, loath, desire or hate, is your brother or sister.

Ω

Conclusion

She conquered her demons and wore her scars like wings.
~Atticus

To my rational minded folks, there are many things you can't see that you believe in, like love, anger, jealousy, envy and lust. Just because you can't physically see another dimension or extraterrestrials doesn't mean they don't exist. Which brings me to another point, if something is meant to be hidden, the very evidence you're looking for has been removed. So, using the concept 'seeing is believing' is outdated and less of an argument than you might think. Measuring something doesn't change its validity. I've forgiven everyone in this story. The more I evolved the less any of it mattered. I became a strong, independent, empathetic girl who loves science. If anyone wanted it proven it was me. I wanted the hard evidence too, but as you can imagine that hasn't been possible yet. Someday, the military will tell the truth, and I won't be some crackpot that created a fantasy. I'll be a person who loved her critics anyway.

Manipulated Memories

I forgave the boys a long time ago, as they were slaves to masters they never really met. The life they've lived is incomplete. So, there's no potential where they can be held responsible for that. Which doesn't mean I'm excusing their actions. I'm compassionate, not stupid. They'll see me as the enemy for a while. And then they'll begin to wake up and remember what really happened.

To the boys' souls and the beings working with them-
I'm glad it was you. We've done this before, and I'd be honored to work with you again. We came here together to show this world what's happening within it, and boy did we. Not everyone will understand why I say this. But the Source of all life, my ancestors, their ancestors and the other men and women who've lived similar lives will.

Earth is a game that we pick the characters for. I chose this. They chose this. No matter the outcome of these events, I would do it all again and wouldn't change a thing. Someday this book will show up on the shelves of the proven impossible. We together have already made history; the world just doesn't know it yet. But our friends in space do.

Survey

I'm interested in your opinions about the subjects in this book. Answer as few or as many questions as you'd like and send them to Missprimordial@gmail.com.

1. Would you want to be contacted by Extraterrestrials?
2. Are you ready for cosmic disclosure?
3. Do you believe alcohol can allow in demons?
4. Do you know someone you would consider to be psychopathic?
5. Do you think they have a soul?
6. Which religion do you think is the most accurate?
7. What do you believe consciousness is?
8. Do you believe you are loved unconditionally by your family?
9. Do you believe there are satanic people worshipping evil?
10. Do you believe in reincarnation?
11. Do you believe people get framed by the police?
12. Do you think the government hides technology from citizens?

Manipulated Memories

13. Do you think you lie to yourself, and you don't even know it?
14. Do you believe in other dimensions?
15. Do you believe people have visions?
16. Where do you think the dream realm is?
17. What do you think happens when you die?
18. Do you think children can see ghosts?
19. Do you think that parents truly know what is best for their children?
20. On a scale of 1 to 10, how important is the truth for you?
21. Do you fear death?
22. Do you always avoid things you fear?
23. What would you do if you could do anything you wanted all day?
24. What do you think stops you from making that happen?
25. First three words when I say fairy tale or mythology.
26. Do you think it's possible the C.I.A and other government entities use children as weapons?
27. Do you believe there is a shadow government?
28. Since we already know police get paid off, how reliable does that make facts?
29. Do you think you are a targeted individual?
30. Do you believe some people enjoy watching pain and suffering?

Manipulated Memories

31. Have you ever asked yourself what evil people do when they assemble?
32. If someone high on drugs came up to you, would you discredit their story right away? Why?
33. What is karma to you?
34. Do you believe the government is hiding what it knows about space travel?

I alone am responsible for the writing and production of this book. I know that I have said things that will ruffle some feathers, and I take full responsibility for that too.
~ Morgan Johnson

Printed in Dunstable, United Kingdom